# JULIUS CAESAR

# JULIUS CAESAR

by Peter David

illustrated by W. T. Mars

Crowell-Collier Press, New York

Collier-Macmillan Limited, London

3944

To the memory of O.T.

Library of Congress Catalog Card Number: 68–10817

The Macmillan Company, New York
Collier-Macmillan Canada Ltd., Toronto, Ontario
Printed in the United States of America

FIRST PRINTING

# CONTENTS

# CAESAR'S ROME

## Chapter One

NEARLY EIGHT HUNDRED YEARS before the beginning of our calendar, so the story went, a boy baby was washed up on the banks of the river Tiber, in central Italy. It was a lonely stretch of land, and the first to come upon the child was a roaming she-wolf that had come down from the hills to drink in the river. The animal took pity on the baby and fed him with her own milk. Later, a shepherd by the name of Faustulus found him, took him home, and raised him as if he were his own son. Faustulus called the boy Romulus.

By the year 753 B.C. Romulus had grown into a man. One morning in April of that year, we are told, the voice of a god moved him to hitch up his plow and to start cutting a furrow through the ground that was soft from the sun. He went on and on through marshes and meadows, until by nightfall he had returned to the place from where he had started. The ring of his furrow enclosed four hundred and fifty acres of land, with seven hills rising a hundred feet and more above the plain. Upon this furrow was built the wall of Rome.

That is the story of the founding of the great city as it was told in Caesar's day, more than six hundred years later. The Romans thought well enough of the story to make a bronze likeness of the she-wolf and to set it up in the Forum, the great square in the center of town. They kept a deep respect for Romulus' great furrow through centuries. Inside it there was to be peace: all citizens had to lay down their arms as they passed the sacred ring and entered the city. And Rome of the seven hills stands to this day.

Romulus' town bred a proud and warlike race and was soon master of all Italy. In the beginning Rome was ruled by kings, but before long the people drove the kings out and founded a republic. This was a deed that the free-spirited Romans recalled with fierce pride, as men in England still remember their Glorious Revolution, and the people of the United States their Declaration of Independence. The Romans now gave the power to make law to a council of elders called the Senate and to the assembled citizens of Rome. The daily business of government and the command of their armies were shared by two Romans chosen for one year. These two were called the consuls, or partners.

Julius Caesar was born in Rome in the year 100 B.C., the only son of an old and noble family. His birthday was most likely the twelfth day of the month which later, in his honor, was called July.

Rome had become the master of the Western world as it was then known, the ruler over one of the greatest empires in all history. Her citizens owned nearly all of the Italian peninsula from its southernmost tip up to the northern plain. They farmed its soil and worked its mines with hundreds of thousands of slaves—prisoners of all races captured in constant warfare. Her armies stood in almost all of the lands that ring the Mediterranean Sea. In Spain and on the Black Sea, in Asia and in Africa, Roman governors collected gold and silver, copper, wine and wheat and oil, and other riches of every sort, and sent them back to the city.

Rome, flooded with the wealth of its provinces, now teemed with a population of over half a million. It was a proud and beautiful city, with great public buildings and temples and theaters, and the splendid town houses of the rich. Great roads ran from the city's gates to her distant outposts, to carry her fighting men swiftly wherever they were needed—roads built so well that many of them are still in use today. Today, too, we may stand and look up at the stone arches of the water lines—

the aqueducts—over which two thousand years ago millions of gallons of water flowed into the city daily, from hills forty miles away, to serve the needs of the householders and the great public baths.

But all through Caesar's childhood and youth, the streets of Rome ran red with Roman blood spilled in civil war. In other days, through centuries of struggle and conquest, the government by the Senate and the people of Rome had served the city well. But once the struggle had been won and Rome had acquired power, the government began to fail. The Romans, who had with their swords subdued the whole known world, now turned their swords against each other and began to fight for the spoils of empire.

No fight is quite as bitter as a fight among brothers. In Caesar's childhood, Rome saw scenes of butchery more savage and more frightful than anything that might happen in battles against a foreign foe. Again and again, there were the sudden torches in the night, the shouting and clash of arms—and then the screams of the dying. Next morning the bloody heads of the victims might be seen in the Forum, hung up to public view by the ruler of the day to strike terror into the hearts of his enemies.

To the subjected peoples in the provinces along the frontiers of the empire, civil war in Rome was a signal to revolt. Rebellion flared up on every side, and hardly a year went by when Roman generals did not lead their legions into battle at the outposts of the empire.

Certainly the greatest of all Roman generals then was Marius, young Caesar's uncle by marriage to his aunt Julia. When the Numidians of North Africa rose up against Roman rule, it was Marius who called together an army, made up for the first time largely of men who made fighting their profession, and put an end to the African rebellion. He returned to Rome victorious, leading the Numidian king Jugurtha in chains before him. Marius next turned north, and with troops he had trained to iron discipline he completely crushed two vast hordes of northern invaders, whose approach had struck all Italy with panic. Proud in his victory, rich in slaves and in booty, and the idol of his troops, he marched back to Rome the savior of the city to make himself its master.

But Marius was a man of battle, not a statesman. The general's attempt to make himself ruler of Rome by force of arms set off a long, confused, and bloody power struggle that almost destroyed the republic. In the end Marius was defeated and driven from the city, and his staunchest supporter, Cinna, was slain by his own troops. The winner in the contest was the aristocrat Sulla—the first Roman to break the ancient law by leading his legions, bristling with arms, across Romulus' sacred furrow into the awestruck, bleeding city.

Sulla let it be known at once that he meant to make full use of the power for which he had staked his life. In 81 B.C. he had himself elected to the office of dictator. This was an ancient institution that the Romans had used often in the past to choose a single leader for a year "in times of grievous wars or serious civil unrest." But with Sulla, the word dictator came to mean much what it means today: the unchecked rule of one man dependent on force of arms, used any way he pleased, and kept just as long as he wished to keep it. Like the dictators of the twentieth century, Sulla now set out to kill the friends and supporters of Marius whom he thought dangerous.

Caesar was now eighteen, a tall, well built, handsome youth. His skin was light, his hair dark, and his black eyes sparkled with intelligence and spirit. He was a splendid rider, skilled with the sword, and a tireless swimmer. His manner was quiet and courteous, his conversation polished, witty, and controlled. The many marble portraits of him that have survived through nearly two thousand years show a wide, firm mouth, a finely curved nose, large eyes, and a remarkably high and wide forehead. Behind that forehead was one of the keenest minds the world has known, an iron will, and unmatched courage. "Caesar was a man of a courage that surpassed human nature," the Roman historian Paterculus tells us, "indeed of a courage greater than man can imagine."

Before Caesar had reached his twentieth year, that courage was put to the test.

Dictator Sulla had every reason to look upon that young nobleman with deep suspicion—he could expect no love or loyalty from Caesar whose uncle Marius he had destroyed. And as if that were not enough, Caesar now refused a marriage his family had arranged, and instead took as a wife the young Cornelia, daughter of the same Cinna who had supported Marius, defied Sulla, and lost his life in the attempt. Marius' nephew and Cinna's daughter—it was as if the spirits of Sulla's most dangerous enemies were gathered together.

Sulla commanded the young Caesar to come before him, and ordered him to divorce Cornelia.

Caesar refused.

These were days when life was cheap, and the life of a man who defied the all-powerful Sulla was even cheaper. Caesar fled from the city in disguise and took to the hills. Slipping from farm to farm in the dark of night, he shook off, for a time, the agents of Sulla who were roaming the country in all directions. Once he was caught; but he paid a bribe to his captor and escaped again.

While he was in hiding, Caesar's family in Rome did not remain idle. Led by his uncle Cotta, they secured an audience with the master of Rome and pleaded for Caesar's life. After all, they begged, he was only a boy, high-spirited, perhaps, and reckless, but not guilty of any crime! And a mere boy could surely not be considered dangerous by mighty Sulla!

Sulla was a man hardened by battle and the daily use of power. He had looked Caesar in the face, and he had looked deep. And he had seen that this young Roman was utterly incapable of fear—even fear of Sulla himself.

"This boy is six times as dangerous as Marius," Sulla replied—but he spared Caesar's life. He merely ordered the family to keep the young man out of the way, perhaps by sending him into the provinces to render military service, as every young Roman did.

So Caesar escaped with his life, and went to Rome's Black Sea province to fight with the armies that were making war on the Parthian king Mithridates.

Not a great deal is known of the years that Caesar spent with the Roman forces in Asia. During his first campaign, we hear, his bravery in battle earned him the Civic Crown, the highest decoration of the Roman army, and from then on he wore a little medal as a reminder of the honor he had gained.

Then, in 79 B.C., Sulla retired. A year later the aged dictator died. Caesar, now twenty-two, thought it safe to return to Rome.

He had seen service on land and sea, and had marched and sailed and fought with the soldiers of Rome, before whom the armies of Asia and the fierce seamen of the Eastern waters had given way. He had gone in and out of the courts of foreign princes and had been honored wherever he went because he was a citizen of Rome, the city that ruled the world.

But as he came back now, after years of absence, he found the city again racked with turmoil and revolt because it was unable to rule itself.

# EARLY YEARS

## Chapter Two

SULLA HAD DONE HARD AND bloody work to give Rome a government such as he thought was needed. He had almost destroyed the power of the People's Assembly, and tried to strengthen the Senate. Nearly five thousand Romans who had resisted him had died at his command. Thousands more fled to Spain, where Quintus Sertorius had set up a government in exile.

But no sooner did Sulla close his eyes than the rule he had meant to establish began to crumble. The Senate, which Sulla had doubled in size—it now counted six hundred members—still showed itself unfit to maintain order. One of the two consuls of the year, a man named Lepidus, reached out to grasp control of the Empire for himself. He invited Caesar to join him. It was a compliment Caesar did not return. "Caesar avoided Lepidus' company," we learn from Paterculus, "even though he was invited with the most attractive promises. For he did not trust Lepidus' character, nor his intelligence."

The Senators, less clear-eyed than Caesar, thought they could buy the ambitious consul off. They offered him a profitable province to administer, and sent him on his way with a large sum of money. But Lepidus never left Italy. Instead, he used the money to raise an army on Italian soil, and marched on Rome. Within sight of the city, he was defeated by forces hastily summoned by the Senate, in a campaign in which the young general Pompey attracted notice. For the moment, Sulla's Senate retained its uncertain hold on power.

Even though Caesar had declined to join in Lepidus' rebellion, he made no secret of it that he held little sympathy for the rule of Sulla's Senate. Within the year, he publicly accused before the courts two leading Romans who had risen to wealth and power under Sulla. One, Dolabella, the late dictator's close friend, had made a fortune in the provinces by extortion; the other, General Hybrida, had grown rich by armed robbery in the Asian campaigns. Both men were let off without punishment, for they had powerful friends in the Senate. Many years later Hybrida was brought to justice. But Caesar had made his mark. His courage in attacking head-on two members of the ruling party attracted notice—but far more did the brilliant skill with which he pleaded his case before the court. Overnight, Caesar was known as one of the truly great speakers of the day.

Still, the experience taught him that his time had not yet come. As a man of the opposition he could not hope to be given a military command where he might show his mettle, for all good posts still went to the supporters of the Sullan party. He resolved to bide his time, and to study more deeply the art of public speaking—the art of moving men to action—which was and is still decisive for success in public life. He resolved to study at the famous school of the most celebrated speaker of the time, Apollonius Molo, on the island of Rhodes.

Rhodes lies some twenty miles off the southwestern coast of today's Turkey, where the Aegean Sea joins the Mediterranean. The shore is mountainous and rocky, the sea peppered with islands large and small. Not far away run the sea-lanes by which the merchant ships with their rich cargo from the Black Sea, from Asia, and from Egypt must pass on their way to the Italian ports.

The men who lived along that coast were born to the sound of the sea, and grew up on ships. They knew every reef and shoal and current, and every bay and harbor where a sailing vessel might find shelter or concealment. It was only natural that at the first sign of Roman weakness they should try their hand at piracy, and prey upon the Roman merchant vessels passing near their waters.

*Such were the men who captured Caesar's ship.*

The historian Plutarch writes with indignation.

"The pirates had arms depots, and harbors, and look-outs, and beacon lights all along the shore. Their fleets were manned with the finest sailors and the most able pilots, and their ships were swift and light, built just right for their task. The power of these pirates was fearful—but even worse was the pride they took in it. Their ships had gilded masts at their stems. The sails were purple cloth, and the oars plated with silver, as if to boast of their evil profession. There was nothing but music and dancing, feasting and celebrations, all along the coast. They captured Roman officers in command of coastal towns, and forced whole cities to pay them taxes—to the shame and the dishonor of Rome."

Such were the men who captured Caesar's ship on its way to Rhodes. The Roman was traveling with a staff of ten slaves and a personal physician. By his company the pirates knew at once that they had made a valuable catch: a noble Roman who could be held for a high ransom. They took him to their island hide-out, and told him that if he wanted to live he would have to pay for his life. The price set was twenty talents.

Twenty talents was a large sum, enough to keep a man in comfort for life. It is characteristic of young Caesar that even at such a moment he thought nothing of money, but much of his honor.

"You fools," he said. "My life is worth at least fifty talents!"

Off to the city of Miletus went all but three of his men to raise the ransom money. Caesar himself stayed behind, "among a set of the most bloodthirsty people in the world," yet his confidence did not leave him. He dealt with the pirates as though they were his servants, not his captors. He joined in their sports and exercises at his pleasure. He ordered them to be quiet when he wished to sleep or study. And he commanded them to listen in silent attention when he read to them the verses or speeches he had composed for practice. The polished language of the Roman was probably not to the taste of these fishermen turned sea-robbers, but when they failed to applaud him Caesar threatened: "You are stupid clods, not worth being alive. As soon as I am free I shall come back—and hang you all!"

Less than two months later he made good his promise. No sooner had he been released on the mainland after the ransom was paid, than he manned several ships and sailed to overtake his captors. He found them still on the same island where he had been their prisoner, and he captured them all. He also took their stolen treasure, repaid his ransom, and distributed the rest among the crews of his ships. The pirates themselves he turned over to Junius, the Roman governor of Asia whose duty it was to bring them to justice.

But Junius, it seems, was himself a pirate—of a different sort. To Caesar he promised that he would think the matter over in good time. But he took no action against them—on the contrary: he cast about for a way to let the pirates escape, in return for a bribe. In those days even Roman governors could be bought. Once more Caesar took matters into his own hands, and ordered the pirates to be treated according to the law: criminals who were not citizens of Rome were put to death by crucifixion. But it is said that Caesar had them killed before they were nailed up, to save them long and cruel suffering. Their dead bodies hung in public view, and a sign on their crosses told of their crime.

Now Caesar could go on to Rhodes and to his studies. "He was wonderfully gifted by nature to become a great statesman and speaker," Plutarch writes. "And he worked painstakingly to improve his natural gifts, until he felt sure that he could at will take second place. Higher he did not aim, because he wanted to be first rather among men of arms."

The call to arms came sooner than expected. Parthian forces invaded the province of Asia which was then only lightly guarded. Caesar broke off his studies in Rhodes, sailed to the mainland, raised his own fighting force, and stopped the Parthian advance until regular Roman troops arrived on the scene.

True, this was not a large campaign. It included no

dramatic battle and yielded no great glory; yet in some ways it was decisive. First, Caesar had shown himself a true Roman by taking up the sword the moment Rome was attacked. Then he had learned something about himself: when he, Caesar, called, men would rally to fight and die for him.

He returned to Rome in the spring of 73 B.C. He was barely twenty-seven. Soon he would be elected to his first public office.

It was the year that saw the outbreak of the last, and the most terrible, revolt of the slaves in Italy, led by Spartacus, a Thracian gladiator. It shook the empire, and is remembered as the War of Spartacus. First, there was just a tiny spark: a band of seventy-eight fighting slaves—they were called gladiators or swordsmen— broke out of a camp near Naples, armed with butcher knives, cleavers, and roasting spits that they had taken from their camp kitchen. The little troop grew into an army of tens of thousands, drawing to itself run-away slaves from the farms, the vineyards, the olive groves, the households of all Italy. For two full years they roamed the country, putting to flight, one by one, the Roman forces sent against them.

Not until 71 B.C. did the Senate decide to call upon Crassus to put an end to the revolt. An able general, Crassus soon cut Spartacus to pieces. General Pompey, just returned from Spain where he had crushed the revolutionary armies of Sertorius, completed the destruction of the slave army. Not more than six thousand slaves lived through the last battle, and they were crucified along the Appian Way, the great road that runs from Rome to the south.

Rome had been saved again from the enemy outside its own walls. But once more, as in the days of Marius and Sulla, two proud generals with their victorious armies were marching toward the city. Would there be another struggle for power within the Roman walls?

The fate of Rome lay in the hands of Crassus and of Pompey. They had no love each for the other, but neither did they know which one of them held the edge of power. Crassus, a man of great ambition and endowed by nature with great personal charm and persuasiveness, was at his best when he was bending men's minds to his will. Pompey, bull-necked man of war, was most popular when he was away on the field of battle, crushing the enemies of the empire. Perhaps they were evenly matched, for they decided to work together. They sent their armies home, and jointly set out to restore the Roman constitution. For some years there was to be peace in the city.

These were years when a man of Caesar's gifts could without bloodshed rise to a position of influence. By 69 B.C., he held a high public office in Rome. Two years later he was on a responsible assignment in the province of Spain. His wife Cornelia had died, and he had married Pompeia, granddaughter of dictator Sulla. The houses of Sulla and of Marius, which only a generation ago had been at daggers' points, were now joined by bonds of marriage. The old rift seemed to be healing.

Again a few years later, Caesar was elected Roman High Priest—an ancient, lifelong office of great honor but with little political power. And in 62 B.C., at last he became praetor—the last step before the highest public office, that of consul. Caesar was rising—how high did he aim?

The story goes that on his way to Spain Caesar and his companions rode through a small, poverty-stricken village in the Alps. Those with him were passing the time with jokes, asking who would want to rule over the miserable little settlement.

"I would much rather be first man among these wretches," Caesar remarked, "than take second place in Rome."

# STATESMAN

*Chapter Three*

IN 60 B.C. JULIUS CAESAR, NOW
forty years of age, presented himself to the Senate and
the people of Rome as a candidate for the highest office
of the state, the office of consul.

Good government had been unknown in Rome for
many years. The Senate, divided by conflicting ambitions,
self-seeking, and careless of the duties inherent in Rome's
power, was all but incapable of action. Also, the Senate
had done all that could be done to lose the goodwill
of the two leading Romans, Pompey and Crassus.

Pompey deserved good treatment from Rome. He
had led Roman armies to victory on three continents.
He had put down an uprising in Africa, defeated the
mutinous consul Lepidus under the walls of Rome,
crushed Sertorius' revolt in Spain, and dealt the final

blow to Spartacus and his fighting slaves. Commanding a Roman fleet of five hundred ships, he had swept the pirates from the Mediterranean Sea, reopened the sea-lanes to trading vessels, and so once more had made food cheap and plentiful in the city. He had stemmed the rising threat of the terrible Parthians in the east, and had defeated their king Mithridates in battle and hounded him to his death. He had carried Roman arms as far as Arabia, and had added large new provinces, including Palestine, to the empire. With it all, he had filled the Roman treasury with gold.

But the flow of gold only sharpened the appetite of

*In 60 B.C. Julius Caesar presented himself to the Senate as a candidate for the office of consul.*

the Senators for personal gain. When Pompey returned victorious from the east, and claimed for his soldiers the wages and the farmsteads that were customary, the Senate could not quite make up its mind to part with land or money for the veterans. Pompey—now called the Great, and famous if ever a Roman was famous—was left to face his legions and to say to them that he, their commander, could not keep the promises he had made to them.

Crassus had equal reason to resent the treatment he received at the hands of the Senators. He was a brilliant financier and the wealthiest man in Rome. But he had also shown brilliance on the field of battle when he beat down Spartacus, before whom other Roman generals had retreated. Like many a noble Roman, Crassus longed for greater military honor. But the Senate steadfastly refused him another military command, probably because it did not want to give military power to a man who already possessed enormous financial power, as well as a great thirst for glory.

Thus the two leading Romans of that day had to stand aside while a weak Senate allowed the empire to drift downhill. Their common misfortune, instead of drawing the two men together, served only to make them more suspicious of each other. It seemed a hopeless moment. Out of this very hopelessness Caesar, and Caesar alone, plucked the great opportunity.

Within a few short months Caesar persuaded Pompey and Crassus to end the feud that had gone on for years, and won them both to his support. Backed by the two men whose very names stood for Rome's military might and wealth, he was elected consul for the year 59 B.C.

The understanding between Caesar, Pompey, and Crassus, which lasted until Crassus' death, came later to be called the first triumvirate—that is, the first alliance of three men to rule the empire. Some men have called it a plot to destroy the Roman republic—or what was left of it. This much is certain: three great Romans, each brilliantly gifted in his own way, joined hands in a time of crisis, and in a peaceful way went about the work of governing the empire, which the Senate could or would not do.

If the Senate was too weak to act, it was yet strong enough to show spite. No sooner had Caesar been elected consul than the Senate passed a special law to strip that office of much of its attraction. For generations it had been the practice to reward a consul at the end of his term of office by making him governor of one of Rome's provinces. But this time, the Senate now announced, the consul was to stay home in Italy when his year was up, and be "commissioner of forests and cattle-runs"—something that today we might call chief ranger. It was honorable work, but to offer it to a man of Caesar's gifts was, and was meant to be, an insult.

But the new consul did not trouble himself about the matter—there was work enough at home. Within a few months, he secured land for Pompey's veterans, even though the Senators stood in his way until he was compelled to go over the Senate's head and appeal to the People's Assembly. One by one, the steps Caesar took during his year in office—always against the stubborn resistance of the Senators—show us that he understood what they were blind to: Rome was no longer a city that had grown rich and powerful by warfare; Rome was the heart, the center, the responsible ruler of a worldwide empire.

Years earlier, we recall, Caesar had raised his voice in public for the first time to call before the court of justice two Roman officers who had used the power of Rome to exploit and to rob subjected peoples. Now consul, he made laws that would punish such robbers severely. He also decreed that all the decisions made by the Senate had to be made public, for every Roman citizen to see. This practice, which men take for granted today, is at the heart of all democratic government: the men who make the laws must give account to the people who gave them their law-making power.

When his year in office ended, Caesar secured, for a term for five years, the post of governor of Cisalpine Gaul. The words mean "Gaul this side of the Alps," the lands in northern Italy between the Alps and the Appenines watered by the Po River. The territory was not then counted among the Roman homelands but was a colony, or province. And soon after, at Pompey's prompting, a second post was given him: he was made governor of another province adjoining to the west, the southern part of today's France which touches the Mediterranean Sea. This was Transalpine Gaul, or "Gaul beyond the Alps," but the French today call it simply Provence—"the province." This part of the empire was the scene of constant uprisings and never-ending trouble, and the man who would govern it must be capable of quick decision and bold action. Caesar had shown that he was such a man.

North and west of Provence, framed by the Pyrenees, the Atlantic Ocean, the English Channel, and the Rhine, lie lands that today are divided among France, Switzerland, and Belgium. They were inhabited by many nations whom the Romans called Gauls—and the name meant terror.

Three centuries before Caesar's time, vast multitudes of Gauls had burst into Italy from beyond the Alps, driven the Roman armies before them like sheep, and taken the city of Rome itself—all but the fortress on Capitol Hill. They killed and looted and finally burned the city around the besieged Capitol. Every young Roman knew the story of how the fierce Gauls scaled the rocks of the Capitol one dark night, and would have taken even Rome's last stronghold by surprise, if the sacred geese of the goddess Juno had not cackled a last minute alarm. In the end, the Gauls had been driven out again— but they remained an ever-present danger, and a large sum of money was set aside in Rome's war chest against the day when the terrible Gauls would invade once more.

The Gauls were a tall race—taller than the Romans, which gave them an advantage in hand-to-hand fighting. They grew beards—the Romans went clean-shaven— and dressed in trousers and sleeved shirts over which they might throw a cloak or more often the skin of an animal to keep warm in their cool, forest-covered country. Gold was plentiful among them, and so they decked themselves out with golden collars, earrings, bracelets, and rings. They fought with the long, two-edged cutting sword, and thus had a reach that was greater than that of the Romans, and with terrible two-bladed battle-axes. Some of them carried pikes eight feet long, with sharp wavy blades. They also used bows and arrows, and slings, and they cast deadly darts. Their shields were wide, their helmets decorated with the horns of animals or tufts of feathers. They took great pride in their swift cavalry. And it was said to be their custom to kill their prisoners and keep the heads as trophies. Before such men, even the proud legions of Rome stood in awe.

"Until the time of Caesar," wrote Cicero, the famous statesman who knew Caesar almost all his life, "until the time of Caesar, our Roman generals thought they had done all that could be done if they just kept the Gauls out of Italy. They thought only of how to stop their attacks, and never dreamed of attacking the Gauls in turn. Even the great Marius never carried war to their towns and homelands, but rested content when he had raised a barrier to stop these torrents of peoples from overflowing all of Italy."

Rome, the proud ruler of the Mediterranean from Spain to the Near Eastern shores, whose name inspired fear in the Greeks, the Parthians, and the Numidians, stood in awe herself before the Gauls—until Caesar came. Cicero continues: "Caesar alone decided to subject Gaul to Roman rule."

# SOLDIER

*Chapter Four*

CAESAR ALONE DECIDED TO SUB-ject Gaul to Roman rule. He alone undertook to make the empire safe against the north.

It was a mighty undertaking, and Caesar himself knew it well. Only now did he seem to rise to his full stature, and to call forth all his powers to meet the task he had set himself. Plutarch tells us:

"From now on, Caesar seems to enter upon a new life. The wars which he now fought showed him to be a soldier and a general as great as the greatest and most admired commanders that ever led an army. We may compare him with any of them—with Sulla, with Marius, and even with Pompey whose fame at that time reached to the very heavens for every excellence in warfare—and we shall find that

Caesar outdid them all. For he had not pursued the war in Gaul a full ten years when he had taken by storm more than eight hundred towns, subdued three hundred nations, and of the three millions of men with whom he fought at various times he had killed one million, and taken prisoner a second."

Caesar himself has left us his account of the vast campaign in a short book known simply as *About the War in Gaul*. To this day the book makes stirring reading. It is written in a style so clear, precise, and simple that even men who had no love for Caesar felt compelled to give it praise. Cicero himself, one of the great masters of language of the ancient world, confessed that he knew of no greater writer than Caesar. And Hirtius, a historian of Caesar's day, wrote with a mixture of admiration and despair: "Caesar set down the facts with the express purpose that someone else might work them up into a history book—but he wrote so beautifully, so flawlessly that no one could do better than Caesar had already done." It is a book which in two thousand years has lost none of its power. Another master of warfare, Napoleon, always kept a copy of it within reach—and so did Napoleon's conqueror, the Duke of Wellington.

The book not only tells about the fighting Caesar did in his conquest of Gaul, but it also tells us much about the man himself, about his quick eye and his quicker mind, which nothing could escape. And most of all it makes us understand why his men fought for him as they had never fought before.

What were they like, Caesar's soldiers, and how did they do battle?

Only a generation ago, a deep change had been worked in the Roman armies by Caesar's uncle Marius. Until that time, Rome's army had been mainly a citizen's army—men who took up arms when they were called, and who went back to their homes and farms and shops as soon as the fighting ended. But as Rome had grown from a city into an empire, more was needed: a standing army of men who made fighting their life's work. Since Marius' day, the Roman legionnaire was a professional fighting man, sworn for a term of many years to follow his general wherever he was called.

An army of such men could be trained to a fighting pitch such as had not been possible before. In peacetime or in war, until they went into battle, the young recruits no less than the seasoned fighters went through tough and thorough practice daily.

Morning and afternoon, the legionnaires practiced their swordsmanship, attacking wooden stakes with wicker shields and wooden foils much heavier than their real weapons. The Roman sword was feared by every nation. Its blade, some twenty inches long, two inches wide, was double-edged and pointed, and could be used to slash and cut, or to thrust and jab. But the slashing blow exposes the raised sword arm to the enemy, and so the Romans practiced the rapid, jabbing thrust as safer, and more deadly.

The Roman shield, made of strong wood covered with leather and edged with iron, was large, square, and curved—shaped somewhat like half a large drum eighteen to twenty inches across. It reached from the shoulders down to the knee, and often had a sharp knob in its center with which a practiced fighter could push and strike the enemy. The Roman helmet, of iron lined with leather, extended down to cover neck and cheeks. So armed, so trained, a legionnaire could go through battle after battle without being wounded. "The Roman soldier," we learn, "looked upon his shield, his sword, and his helmet as parts of his body."

Next to the sword, the Romans' most deadly weapon of attack was the javelin, cast with superb marksmanship learned in daily practice. The use of bows and arrows, stone slings, and darts was something which the Romans left mostly to the foreign troops accompanying the legions—the lightly armed soldiers drawn from Africa and the islands of the Mediterranean. The slingers learned to swing their weapon only once around their heads before the throw, to keep the moment when they stood exposed to the missiles of the enemy as short as possible.

*They knew their leader as a man who knew each one of his men.*

All practiced cutting trees—for camp stockades, siege engines, bridges; digging ditches; swimming in river, lake, and sea; and the march, the quick-step, and the run under full arms and in all kinds of weather. They fought sham battles. And in the circus they watched the games in which the fighting slaves of other nations fought for their lives, to learn how a Gaul, a German, or a Parthian fights—and how to defeat him. When their general called them, they were prepared.

A Roman soldier in battle dress went with his arms bare or only lightly clothed, to give him freedom of movement. His shoulders, chest, back, waist, and hips were protected by a cuirass, or leather bodkin, covered with metal scales to make it strong. His legs from knee to ankle were shielded by iron shin guards. His sword hung from his left, ready to be drawn with his right hand after he had thrown the javelins which he carried into battle. As Caesar's men won victory after victory, and were given a share in the spoils more generous than the troops of any other commander, their armor grew in splendor: their helmets, shields, and sword buckles were often inlaid in gold and silver. A parade of such troops was a proud and dazzling sight, and their glittering charge into battle would try the stoutest courage.

They usually formed for battle in large squares sixteen to twenty men deep, the soldiers spaced six feet or more apart to give them room to throw their javelins. A Roman legion in battle formation presented to the enemy a front one mile or more in width.

Caesar followed the custom of drawing his troops up

on the gentle slope of a hill whenever possible, to give them an advantage in throwing their javelins, and in charging down upon the enemy when the time came. There they stood almost motionless, a wall of defiance, daring the others to attack. And the barbarians, their great courage raised still higher because they most often outnumbered the Romans five or even ten to one, rushed upon them.

When the attackers came within three hundred paces, the Roman wall began to move. The legionnaires moved forward, slowly at first, marching in step—within a hundred paces of the enemy they broke into a run—and then, at twenty paces, the first two ranks let fly their javelins in a deadly volley.

Most often this terrifying charge broke the enemy's front. The second rank of men now moved up to fill the intervals in the first. Advancing as a body, with swords drawn, they now pressed in upon a disorganized opponent. The outcome of many a battle was decided by Caesar's legionnaires in those first few moments after they had cast their javelins and drawn their swords.

The Gauls bled, and learned. They, too, now advanced in a solid line, their large shields overlapping so that they resembled the tightly joined scales in the shell of a tortoise—indeed, tortoise is the name the Roman soldier gave to that formation. In return, the Romans, accomplished marksmen, now aimed their javelins squarely at the overlapping edges of the Gallic shields—and wherever a javelin hit true, two shields were pinned together and so made useless: two Gauls were defenseless before the Roman swords.

The full power and skill of Roman arms came into play when the enemy stood firm under the first volley of javelins thrown at close range. If the missiles of the first two Roman ranks made no dent in the enemy's formation, these ranks fell back while the next two took their place. There was no loss in their order—the spaces between men gave ample room for advance and return. Now the next two lines discharged their javelins, and then the next—the ten-line Roman troop could deliver five deadly volleys in rapid succession. The light troops meanwhile kept the legionnaires supplied with missiles. Each block within the legion held its ground—but within each block, the legionnaires moved back and forth in dancelike, weaving motion, delivering volley after volley. The same motion continued after they had joined in hand-to-hand combat: when the first fighting line ceased gaining on the enemy, the second line, held back until now two hundred feet or more, went forward and took its place. All lines could in this way come gradually into action, taking their turn and at times fighting all day until they carried the battle. The Roman legion surely was one of the most formidable fighting machines in all the history of warfare.

But Caesar's legions were far more than a mere machine. If arms and training gave them power and precision, it was their general who gave them their spirit and their pride. They knew their leader as a man who shared with them every danger and every discomfort; who was generous with them to the point of folly; who knew each one of his men and judged him by his battle record and by nothing else—a general who combined unmatched caution with unmatched daring, and who never lost a battle. Plutarch, once more, has summed it up: "Caesar enjoyed the loyalty and devotion of his soldiers to such a degree that men who in other battles were just ordinary soldiers, showed a courage that knew no defeat and suffered no resistance when the time came to fight for Caesar's glory."

# THE FIRST CAMPAIGN

## Chapter Five

ALARMING NEWS WAS COMING
to the city from the north. The provinces beyond the
Alps were threatened by a danger as dreadful as that
which only the fighting genius of Marius had stopped
a generation earlier: the German nations from beyond
the Rhine were threatening invasion.

In fact, the invasion was even now under way. One
of the Gallic nations, at war with its neighbor, had called
the powerful German king Ariovistus across the Rhine
for help. The German came, with fifteen thousand of
his warriors. He took a liking to the land in which he had
been invited to do battle, and made up his mind to stay.
As a beginning, he took over one-third of the territory
of his Gallic employer in payment for his services. He
now drove out the native settlers, and brought in larger

*The whole Swiss nation set out on the great trek.*

and larger numbers of his own countrymen. By the year 58 B.C., the German population in the heart of Gaul had grown well past a hundred thousand.

Nor was this all. Other German nations were pressing hard upon the Swiss south of the Rhine, in the mountainous territories between Lake Constance and Caesar's Provence. The Swiss, a hardy folk with all the toughness of mountaineers, had long stood off German pressure, but when they could bear it no longer, they began to look for a more peaceful land elsewhere. In 58 B.C. they made up their minds to migrate across Gaul to Aquitaine—what is today southwestern France—where they would find mountains as beautiful and rugged as those among which they were born, and grazing lands for their cattle.

After many months of preparation, the whole Swiss nation set out on the great trek. Three hundred and sixty eight thousand men, women, and children, with thousands of carts carrying enough flour to last them for three months, and leading their cattle behind them, left their homes and moved west. They were to meet on March 28, at winter's end, on the banks of the Rhone River, and there cross over into Roman territory. Their hearts were set on their new home ahead. To do away with any thought of turning back, they destroyed all they left behind: twelve towns, four hundred villages, and thousands of homesteads went up in flames.

A nation on the march, in need of food during its slow advance, must live off the country through which it passes. But this country was now under Caesar's care, and he would not allow it to be stripped and looted. Besides, the Swiss lands left behind were sure to fill up at once with Germans, and the Roman did not want them for neighbors of his province.

In eight days' hard riding, Caesar hastened from Rome to Lake Geneva, where the Swiss would attempt to cross over. He found on the spot one single legion—the Tenth, with hardly more than five thousand men—with which to deny passage to the Swiss nation whose fighting force numbered close to one hundred thousand. But the Swiss, weighed down with baggage and livestock, were moving slowly. He still had a few weeks left.

Caesar at once called for his three legions south of the Alps, and in addition began to raise two new legions. Meanwhile, the seasoned men of the Tenth Legion put away their swords and took up pick-axe and spade. And when the Swiss columns began to arrive, a week or two later, they found their passage blocked. Along a stretch of eighteen miles, from the lake to the Jura Mountains in the north, the legionnaires had thrown a trench over which no wagon train could cross. And behind it, there now rose a wall sixteen feet high, studded with fortified points, on which the Roman soldiers stood guard.

The Swiss turned north. Although Caesar had denied

them passage, they would by-pass the Roman province and march instead through central Gaul.

Caesar, his army now swelled to six legions, or about thirty thousand men, followed. He dogged their steps, but did not yet seek battle. Two of his legions were untried recruits.

Weeks later, his scouts reported that the Swiss had reached the Saone River at a point some twelve miles ahead, and were crossing it on a bridge built of boats and rafts. Caesar set out at midnight, taking half his force. At dawn he was upon them.

Three-fourths of the Swiss nation had crossed the river when the legions of Caesar appeared on the scene. Caesar at once attacked the quarter that was still on the near bank. Their fighting force greatly outnumbered his, and they fought bravely as the Swiss have always done. But they could not outfight him. Only a few of them escaped into the hills and woods—the rest died there. We know exactly the place where Caesar fought his first great battle in the Gallic War: Napoleon III, Emperor of France, in 1862 sent scholars to dig at the spot Caesar described in his book "about the war in Gaul." As the French spades cut into the earth they brought to light an immense number of human bones—the skeletons of men, women, children—and of broken ornaments and weapons.

The battle over, Caesar's engineers went to work. They

had no power other than the muscles of the legionnaires, and no materials but what they found on the spot. For them, it was enough—they threw a bridge across the river in a single day.

The surviving Swiss on the far side of the river were struck with awe as they watched the Romans at work. Who could resist these strangers who, between dawn and dusk, could build a bridge far better than what they, the Swiss, had needed twenty days to do?

Soon Swiss messengers arrived in Caesar's camp to sue for peace. But the gallant little nation was still un-

*The Roman formed his four veteran legions in three lines.*

willing to bow to Caesar's demand that they return to their homelands. They would march on, they warned him, and the seventy thousand fighting men they had left would defend them to the end.

Caesar, still cautious, followed them again. For more than ten days the two columns moved along one behind the other. Caesar's soldiers no longer feared the Swiss. Caesar's two new legions hardened, but the Swiss refused to give battle.

Now the food supplies of the Roman legions began to run low. The time was only two days off when each of

Caesar's soldiers was to receive his two-weekly ration of twenty-five pounds of wheat. Caesar decided to abandon the pursuit for the time being, and to make sure first that his troops were well supplied. He turned aside from the trail of the Swiss and made for the town of Bibracte, a Gallic stronghold sixteen miles away and richly stocked with grain.

A deserter from among the Gallic horsemen who were with Caesar informed the Swiss of the sudden change of marching orders. But neither he nor they understood Caesar's reasons. They thought that Caesar was at last giving up the chase and was retreating.

If the Swiss had so far avoided battle with the Romans, they now took courage. Being pursued no longer, they wheeled about and in their turn gave chase to the Roman troops. Soon the horsemen of the Swiss advance were harassing Caesar's rear guard. Caesar's moment had come.

Leaving his baggage train under the protection of his two new legions, the Roman halted on a nearby hill, formed his four veteran legions in three lines along the slope, and offered battle. As the Swiss host drew close, Caesar rode along his front and addressed his men, reminding them of their proud tradition. His battle horse, legend tells us, was a most wonderful animal with feet that looked almost human, each hoof being cloven in five parts as if it had five toes. Much later, he would have a likeness of it made in bronze and set up in Rome, in the Temple of Venus. But on this day, we know, he dismounted and sent his horse away. A man on horseback can escape if things go wrong. Caesar would stay with his troops and share every danger with them.

Meanwhile, the Swiss had drawn up their carts in a circle on low ground nearby, much as early American settlers, when in Indian territory, placed their covered wagon trains in a circle for the night. The Swiss left their women and children inside the enclosure, with fifteen thousand of their troops to guard them. Then they massed together in the solid phalanx that was their customary battle order, interlocked their shields in front, along their flanks, and over their heads, and charged the Romans at a run.

The first volley of Roman javelins tore gaps in the Swiss ranks. The second slowed their advance. Now the Romans drew their swords and fell to. Soon the Swiss had to give ground. Still in good order, they retreated to a hill three-quarters of a mile away, and there made a stand.

The Roman legions followed in hot pursuit. As they advanced, they passed and left behind them the Swiss detachment that was guarding the wagon circle. This guard now fell upon them from behind and attacked the Roman rear with the utmost fury in an attempt to save the day.

Caught from two sides, Caesar faced his third line about and fought in both directions. From noon until night fell the battle wavered, and grew in bitterness. Caesar mentions with admiration that all day long not a single Swiss had turned his back upon the Romans. But as darkness came, the Swiss were forced to yield and to retreat within the circle of their carts. There they cast their spears and javelins from above, or crawled between the wheels and fought from below with their long pikes. Even the women and the children joined in the fighting. The slaughter lasted deep into the night before Swiss courage broke.

Three hundred and sixty eight thousand strong they had left Switzerland. Only a hundred and thirty thousand survived the battle of Bibracte. These, at Caesar's command, now wandered back to the country they had left behind. Once they had yielded to his demands he protected them, and made sure that they were given safe conduct and food on their way home. The Roman historian Florus described it well: "Caesar drove this people back into their country as if he were a shepherd driving his flock back into the fold."

# THE GERMANS

## Chapter Six

NEWS OF THE BATTLE RAN through Gaul. From all the Gallic nations messengers arrived to render homage to the victor, and to lay before him their urgent plea that he help them out of their common danger: the German invasion. The Gallic princes met before Caesar to tell how the German intruder, King Ariovistus, was growing more demanding and more arrogant each day. He had taken their children captive, and threatened to torture them. Just a few months before, he had been joined by another twenty-four thousand Germans, and even now vast German forces were gathering beyond the Rhine and preparing for the crossing. If he were not stopped soon, he would drive all the Gauls out of their country—just as the Swiss had been driven out—and flood the land with Germans.

The Roman listened thoughtfully and then dismissed the princes of Gaul. Caesar tells us that he felt ashamed to think that the people of Gaul, friends of Rome, should live in fear of a foreign tyrant. He then sent messengers to King Ariovistus, inviting him to meet halfway between their camps in order to discuss matters of high importance to them both.

The king's reply left nothing to the imagination: "If I wanted anything from you, Caesar, I would come to you," the proud German answered. "If you want anything from me, you can come to me. But let me warn you not to bring your armies into that part of Gaul which is mine, mine because I have taken it by force of arms!"

Caesar's second message was equally clear: "I am making of you three requests. First, you will bring no more German forces across the Rhine. Second, you will set free the hostages taken from the Gallic princes. Third, you will stop making war on the friends of Rome among the nations of Gaul. If you do so we shall be friends. If not, then I, the governor of this province, shall know how to protect it."

This was an ultimatum. Without a moment's hesitation, the German answered back: "I do not take orders from you. To this day, I have destroyed anyone who has made war on me. Attack me any time you wish, and you will find out for yourself what my men are like: they never lost a war, they are trained to perfection, they have

*The Germans are fierce and savage fighters.*

not been sheltered under a roof for fourteen years."

This answer left no room for further talk. Caesar broke camp and marched. On the way, he learned that the German was moving toward the city of Besançon, a Gallic stronghold filled with large stores of supplies. In forced marches of a speed until then unheard-of, he reached the city first. There he made camp to let his own baggage train catch up. Meanwhile, he sent out scouts to learn all he could about his enemy.

Caesar's legionnaires, too, wanted to know as much as possible about the Germans whom they had never before met in battle. Full of questions, they crowded around the Gallic traders visiting the camp. At once, fearful tales were being spread through the Roman tents: the Germans are all giants; they are incredibly well trained; they are fierce and savage fighters whom no one can resist; the terrible piercing stare of their eyes alone is enough to make you turn and run!

The untried recruits among the Roman army panicked. Their terror spread. Some of the young Roman noblemen who had come along on the campaign for the sake of adventure suddenly found that they had urgent business at home, and left, while others hid tearfully in their tents and wrote their wills. Caesar's trusted officers told him that his armies would follow him no farther into this unknown, treacherous, and hostile country.

There are many proud tales in history of how one man's

high courage outdid the courage of another. But there is none to match the story of how Caesar overcame the fear in his own camp. He called before him all his officers, down to those who commanded not more than a hundred men, and spoke to them:

"Why are you down-hearted?" he said. "The Germans whom we shall fight—are they not the same people whom Marius defeated, and did he not defeat them with an army made up of Romans just like ourselves? Even the Swiss have often fought the Germans, and very often beaten them. And the Swiss, you remember, could not stand up against us!

"I am told that my men will not obey my marching orders. I do not believe it. No army has ever refused to obey its general unless he was incompetent, dishonest, or miserly with his troops. As concerns my character, my whole life is my witness. What I am worth as a leader in battle the Swiss campaign has shown.

"I had meant to stay here for a few more days. But now I have decided to march tomorrow. We shall strike camp between three and six o'clock in the morning. Then we shall see who follows me. Even if no one else follows, I shall still march with the Tenth Legion, whose courage I need not doubt. The Tenth will be my bodyguard."

Caesar neither pleaded, nor blamed, nor threatened. He spoke to them as men, and in his words his legions found their fighting hearts. When he rode out of camp at three o'clock the next morning, they followed to a man, eager and confident to fight, proud of their leader.

They marched continuously for six days, until his scouts told Caesar that he was almost within striking distance of Ariovistus and his army, who were encamped close to the Rhine.

Startled by Caesar's lightning approach, the German king now asked for a conference. The two men met on horseback on a hilltop, halfway between their camps, and talked. Each came escorted by a bodyguard of cavalry.

*The two men met on horseback.*

But neither yielded, and so they parted. The war was on. The two opponents moved their camps close to each other, and made ready for the final test.

For five days running, Caesar drew up his forces and offered battle. But the German main force remained inside their wagon train encampment—only the German horsemen made daily sallies to harass the Romans who were strengthening their camp. There were six thousand German riders, and each had with him his own foot soldier. These foot soldiers, picked for their speed and cour-

age, had in long training learned to keep pace with the horse advancing at a gallop by running alongside and clinging to its mane. They were a formidable fighting force that the Romans could oppose only with the cavalry of their Gallic allies.

A prisoner taken in one of the cavalry skirmishes at last explained why Ariovistus was delaying battle: his soothsayers had told him that if he wished to win he must not fight before the moon was new. This was enough—Caesar decided to force battle at once.

The next day, the whole Roman force drew up in open battle order and, leaving their own camps but lightly guarded, advanced upon the German encampment. Ariovistus saw that he would have to meet the attack or else he would be assaulted in his wagon train. His men sallied forth, massed in groups of three or four hundred, joined their shields in front and overhead in tortoise formation, and charged the Roman legions with such speed that there was no time to cast the javelins. The Romans drew their swords and joined battle. As the two fronts crashed against each other, Caesar proudly tells us, some of his legionnaires leaped upon the wall of German shields, tore the shields away by sheer force, and stabbed at the enemy from above.

Caesar himself, wearing his scarlet cloak that marked him out in battle, led the right wing. From the wagons behind the German host, the women called out encouragement to their husbands, fathers, and brothers, imploring them to fight well and to save their families from death or Roman slavery.

For a long while the outcome hung in the balance. But the legionnaires pressed on—and all at once the Germans lost heart. Their army turned and fled.

What began as a rout ended as a massacre. The Romans gave pursuit and drove the enemy before them right to the banks of the Rhine, which was twelve miles away. Only a few of the Germans tried to swim the great river, or found boats and so made their escape—among them Ariovistus himself. The others died under the Roman swords, or lost their freedom.

Beyond the Rhine, the German nations who had gathered for the crossing learned of the disaster from the few survivors. They turned around, disbanded, and went home.

It was now mid-September 58 B.C. Within that one short spring and summer of his first year in Gaul, Caesar had waged and won two great campaigns. He had repulsed the Swiss, and had crushed the German armies that had crossed the Rhine. But this, he knew, was only the beginning. The Gauls had helped, or at least had not opposed, him while he was fighting to drive off their enemies; but they would just as readily turn against him when it suited their purpose. A country such as Gaul, he knew, could not be secured in one year's campaigning.

Caesar prepared. Sooner than the turn of seasons required, he led his victorious army back to winter quarters, in the very heart of Gaul. It was the first time in history that Roman troops stayed through the winter in that country; until now, all Roman expeditions had withdrawn to the province in the south when the campaigning season was at an end. Caesar himself returned across the Alps to attend to the government of his Italian provinces, and to raise two new legions in preparation for the coming storm.

# THE BELGIAN REVOLT

## Chapter Seven

THE STORM BROKE IN THE SPRING of 57 B.C. All through that winter intelligence had reached Caesar that the Belgian nations in the north of Gaul, between the English Channel and the lower Rhine, were banding together in a vast alliance against Rome. When May came, Caesar rejoined his forces in central Gaul, arranged for supplies to be brought up, broke camp, and marched. Before the month had ended, his legions were on their way north.

Scouts and informers soon began to bring him alarming news: the forces raised against him were vaster than any he had yet encountered. The Belgians, famed for their warlike spirit, had put on foot two hundred and ninety-six thousand of their best fighting men. Caesar's own army numbered, at best, fifty thousand.

Caesar drove on and entered enemy territory. In striking distance of the Belgian host, he threw his force across the strategic river Aisne, and set up a bridgehead on the other side, fortified by a huge wall and ditch.

Behind him were all the nations of Gaul—allies of the moment, but ever ready to betray him if he should show signs of weakness. Before him, encamped less than two miles away, lay the Belgian armies. At night, their watch fires could be seen glowing in the distance, along a front eight miles in length. It was a time for caution, and Caesar was content to await his chance.

It was not long in coming. The Belgian host, commanded by a dozen self-willed princes rather than by one master, had failed to provide adequate supplies. After two spiritless attacks on Caesar's camp, both easily repulsed by the legionnaires, they decided to disband. As quickly as they had come together, they now just as quickly broke up and marched their various ways. In parting they vowed to come to each other's aid wherever the Roman should make his first attack.

They would not meet again. As soon as Caesar learned their purpose, he gave pursuit. The next day, a lightning march of twenty-eight miles brought him to the ramparts of the Belgian stronghold at Soissons. It was too well defended to be taken by assault without the aid of engines. His engineers began their work. With amazement and growing fear, the Belgians watched from their fortress as mantlets, galleries, battering rams, and huge siege towers began to rise with unbelievable speed. Before the siege had yet begun, they sued for peace. Caesar accepted their surrender and marched on against his next objective, the fortress at Beauvais. Even before he had arrived there, he was met by the elders of the tribe, who threw themselves on his mercy. Yet another nation laid down their arms in terror of his approach. Then Caesar turned northeast to meet the Nervii, a large and gallant nation.

He had driven deep into the lands of the Nervii and was building his first camp there, above the banks of the Sambre River, when they fell upon the Roman army at a position which only an army with the boldest courage would attack. In full force they broke out of a woods beyond the river, swarmed down the slope and across the stream, and raced up the hill on which the Roman camp was rising, "with such extraordinary speed, it seemed as though they were doing all this at one and the same moment."

Caesar had never been closer to defeat than in the battle at the Sambre River. Perhaps this is why he described the confused and furious action with such fullness and in such living detail. Through his words, we can see him in the thick of battle, now at this danger spot, now at another, here regrouping hard-pressed units to the attack, there shouting courage to his commanders by name, now snatching up the shield of a wounded soldier and joining the fighting in the front rank. It was hours of hot fighting until the fortunes of battle turned and the onslaught of the Belgians was halted. Forced into the defensive, the Belgians fought on until the end. To these, his fiercest enemies, Caesar has paid a tribute such as he gave no other:

"The enemy's position was by now completely without hope. But their courage was beyond belief. We cut down their front ranks—but those behind stepped on the bodies of their fallen comrades and fought on from there. When they, too, died, and bodies piled upon bodies, the next rank leaped up on the pile and from up there cast down their own javelins, or returned those we were throwing at them. They were a people of a courage that does not have its like: a courage that carried them across a broad river and up the steep embankments on the other side, and then made them rush our strong defensive position. Their spirit must have been very great."

And the final sentence rings with honest sorrow for so gallant an enemy: "So ended the battle by which the name and the nation of the Nervii was wiped out."

There was one more task ahead. A day's march downstream, where the Sambre flows into the Meuse, large Belgian forces were in a fortress made almost unassailable by hills and the two rivers. Caesar moved up, cut off all escape on the land side by a wall and ditch five miles long, and once more set his men to building the siege engines he needed, within sight of the beleaguered Belgians though out of range of their missiles.

At first, the Belgians felt safe within their walls, and merely laughed as they saw the battering rams and siege towers take shape below under the skilled hands of the Romans. "What are you going to do with that big tower way over there?" they shouted. "You don't think you can move it, you skinny little men?" But soon the tower was finished, and began to move closer and closer. It was a sight none of them had ever seen, and it stopped their laughter and froze them with fear. "You Romans must have the help of spirits from the other world," they now called. "We cannot fight against spirits. Be merciful, and we will surrender!"

Caesar replied that if they handed over their arms before his battering rams had touched their walls, their lives and their liberty would be safe. The Belgians agreed, and weapons rained down from the fortress walls into the ditches below. But secretly they kept a good part of their arms, and in the night made a desperate attempt to break out, in the hope that Caesar's watchfulness had been ended by their apparent surrender.

The Romans easily drove them back within the walls. Next day, the battering rams crashed through the walls and gates. The fortress had fallen.

There was no mercy for treachery. "I sold the whole

*Caesar prepared to assault the Belgian fortress.*

population of the town as slaves, in one batch," Caesar reports bluntly. "I later heard there were fifty-three thousand of them."

It was now August. Within a little over three months, Caesar had broken the Belgian alliance. Those whom he had not fought now surrendeded without a blow. As the year drew to a close, Caesar could report to Rome that "there was every reason to believe that all Gaul was now at peace." When his dispatches reached the city, the

Romans proclaimed a public
thanksgiving that lasted fifteen days.
No Roman had ever been so honored.

But Caesar had not reckoned with the headstrong
nations in northwestern France, inhabiting the blunt peninsula that juts out into the Atlantic Ocean south of the
English Channel. Today the region is known as Brittany,
and its inhabitants are known as Bretons. The Bretons
had surrendered without a fight, in the first shock of

terror that Caesar's rapid victories in the north cast over all of Gaul.

The Seventh Legion was quartered for the winter in Brittany. Two of its officers, foraging for food, were taken captive by one of the Breton nations. Other Roman officers met with the same fate. This was a very serious breach of peace. The guilty Bretons quickly realized that Rome would not take the matter lightly. They looked for help in the day of reckoning ahead. In this way, more than half a dozen Breton nations allied themselves in the winter months of 57 to 56 B.C. to defy the Romans.

This alliance was not as foolhardy as it might seem on first thought. The Bretons were seafaring people, accustomed to sailing the rough and dangerous waters of the Atlantic Ocean. Their ships crossed freely back and forth between their own harbors and those of Britain. Their fortified towns, built far out in the sea on the points of spits of land or promontories, were well-nigh unassailable, as they seemed to rise and sink with the change of the tides. For several hours twice a day—at high tide—they were protected on all sides by the waters lying around them like a huge moat. No ship could safely reach them that was not steered by a skilled pilot who knew each reef and shoal and current. And the Bretons knew themselves to be much better and more daring sailors than the Romans—those Romans whose seamanship was only good enough for the quiet waters of the landlocked Mediterranean, where the change of tides could barely be noticed, and where the raging storms and towering breakers of the open sea were unknown.

When Caesar first heard of the Breton conspiracy in mid-winter, he began to make preparations for a form of warfare new and unfamiliar to him. He gathered shipwrights and sailors throughout his provinces, and set them to building a fleet in the Loire River, which flows into the Atlantic south of the Breton coast. With the return of spring he was back in Gaul, attacking the Bretons on land while waiting for the completion of his fleet. More than one of the sea-locked Breton strongholds fell to him: his engineers built pairs of huge breakwaters from the coast to the fortress walls, locking out the Atlantic tides and allowing his siege towers to move up and do their work of destruction. But when his troops at last burst into the conquered stronghold from the land side, they found it deserted. Again and again, the enemy escaped by ship out into the sea, taking their stores with them. Without a fleet, Caesar could not force a decision.

At last his ships were ready and came swarming down the Loire and into the open waters. They were the fast and agile vessels of the Romans, such as Pompey had used to sweep the pirates from the Mediterranean Sea. They were low along the sides, as well as in stem and stern, to let their cargo of legionnaires readily swarm aboard an enemy ship to which their grappling hooks made fast. Their prow was sharp and strong, to ram and sink the enemy, but they were otherwise lightly built, to gain them speed. They had no sails but shot along swiftly to the rapid, rhythmic beat of long ranks of oars handled by practiced rowers.

The ships of the Bretons were built for the rough Atlantic. They were made of oak, with crossbeams a foot thick, and bolted together with iron spikes as thick as a man's thumb. Their bottoms were flatter than those of the Roman ships, so that they could ride over shallows or close to the shore, and could be beached at low tide to float again as the high tide returned. Their sides were high against the wash of the ocean waves, and their stems and sterns, made to cut through the heaving billows of the sea, towered above those of the Roman ships almost beyond javelin range. They had no oars but moved by sails made of thin leather to withstand the violent gales that churn the Atlantic.

The two fleets met in the Bay of Quiberon. As the Romans approached, the Bretons confidently sailed out of the jagged recesses of the rocky coast and formed for battle. They outnumbered the Roman ships two to one or more, and could be confident of victory.

But the Roman vessels had aboard a strange tool, made at the command of Decimus Brutus, leader of the fleet: a large, sharp hook, shaped like a sickle, fastened to the end of a long, thick pole.

*One vigorous pull and the Breton ropes snapped.*

While Caesar and his land forces watched from the hills along the shore—the place is known today as St. Jacques' Point—the Roman ships darted to the attack. They raced alongside a Breton ship. Their hooked poles shot out and grasped the ropes that held the yardarms to the masts of the enemy; the Roman rowers threw themselves into the oars with all their strength: one vigorous pull and the Breton ropes snapped. The yards collapsed and left the Breton ship helpless.

With this device, the sailors of Brutus' fleet put the Breton ships out of action one by one. Soon the Breton ships that still had the use of their sails turned about and tried to find safety in the crannies of the ragged coast. But the wind had died down. The Breton vessels, scattered in their attempted flight, lay helpless upon the becalmed sea. One after the other, the Romans overpowered and destroyed them, until at last the falling of night set an end to the slaughter.

Thus in one day the entire Breton fleet, the whole strength of the Breton nations, was wiped out. All their best fighting men had been on those ships—and not more than a handful escaped death or slavery. The rest of the nations surrendered, only to meet the same fate. If Caesar's patience and forbearance toward his enemies were famous in later years, in this campaign he acted with exceeding harshness. But the event served notice on all Gaul that Rome would not tolerate revolt.

# THE RHINE,
# THE CHANNEL,
# AND THE
# KING OF GAUL

*Chapter Eight*

FROM THE RHINE TO THE ENG-
lish Channel, all Gaul now bowed to Caesar's power and
offered treaties of peace.

But on the far side of the Rhine were large and powerful German nations, forever restless, forever crowding
in upon the smaller tribes that lived along the river
until they were forced to cross and seek new homes in
Gaul. And from across the English Channel, help had
come and would come again to the coastal nations of Gaul
that had risen against Rome. As long as the princes of
Britain and of Germany felt safe behind their water barriers, which the Roman could not or dared not cross, they

meant a standing threat to his rule in Gaul. In 55 B.C., Caesar resolved to show them that neither river nor ocean channel would stop his armies.

First, they advanced to the Rhine. In mid-June, Caesar's legionnaires stood once again on the banks of the river into which three years earlier they had thrown Ariovistus and his German forces. Caesar's Gallic allies now eagerly offered to supply the large fleet of boats which, they thought, he needed for the crossing. Caesar declined. For this great undertaking he meant to rely on his own strength alone.

The Rhine, one of the great rivers of the European continent, draws its water from half a dozen countries. Until Caesar came, its lower and middle reaches had never yet been bridged.

Caesar selected for the crossing a point close to the place where today rises the city of Bonn. The width of the river here is well over a quarter of a mile, the current rapid, and the riverbed deep. Even with all the resources of modern technology—with all our steel and steam and power engines—it is no small feat to throw a bridge across such a river. Caesar had only the timber that grew along the river's edge, and his legions. And yet, within ten days after the first Roman axe had cut into the first tree, the bridge stood completed.

In less than a page Caesar tells how it was done, and his description is so alive and clear that we can see the structure growing under our eyes. A pair of piles, each a foot and a half thick, is sunk from rafts into the river-bed, leaning a little with the current—and forty feet downstream, leaning against the current, another such pair. Now the two pairs are joined by a crossbeam two feet wide, so that they form a trestle. A series of these trestles is set up side by side across the whole width of the river. Now beams are laid from one trestle to the next, and over them poles, branches, brush—and there is the road on which the legions march across the water. Downstream, more piles brace the bridge against the current; upstream, other piles shield the trestles against tree trunks or weighted ships that the Germans might send down the river to destroy the bridge.

No blood was spilled in this show of Roman power, and yet it was one of Caesar's great victories. The German nations along the far bank of the Rhine hastened to send messengers to offer friendship and peace, or else vanished into the uncharted forests of their country. Caesar left a strong guard at the bridgeheads, explored the German lands for a short while, and then withdrew, breaking the bridge behind him.

Next he went to the coast of the English Channel. Here Caesar brought together the fighting ships with which the year before he had defeated the Bretons. Besides, he ordered the construction of eighty transport vessels—enough to carry two of his legions. On August

*And there is the road on which the legions march across the water.*

26, he sailed. It was by now much too late in the year to think of an extended exploration of the British island; but there was time enough to find out what he would need to know about the country and its peoples for next year's full-scale invasion. Before the end of September, Caesar was back in Gaul. Storms had damaged his fleet; he had lost a number of men; winds and tides had cut off his cavalry ships and thrown them back into the harbors of Gaul. But he had observed much, and what he had seen he could now put to use.

In mid-July 54 B.C. Caesar set out again. This time his fleet numbered close to eight hundred ships, six hundred of them specially designed transports. He had observed that in the Channel the waves do not rise as high as in the open waters of the ocean, and so had his ships built low along the sides to make for easy loading and unloading of his cavalry. The ships were broader than the Roman model, and had flat bottoms so that they could readily be run up onto the beaches. When the French emperor Napoleon, in the year A.D. 1804, built a fleet to invade England, he followed the design that Caesar had developed for the same purpose.

The Roman ships, driven by both oars and sails, left from their harbor near Boulogne on July 20, and touched the English coast some ten hours later. The English, who the year before had fiercely resisted Caesar's landing, withdrew at the sight of so vast a fleet, and Caesar landed unopposed with five legions and two thousand horsemen.

He returned after little more than a month—after battle, labor, and near disaster. Although he had encountered and defeated one of the most powerful British kings, he had learned that it would not be easy to conquer Britain.

The British, Caesar reported, were far more dangerous enemies than the Gauls. The went to battle painted blue—their skin dyed with the juice of woad, a mustard plant—to frighten their opponents. They were taller than the Gauls, and covered themselves with animal skins. They used long swords, and small bucklers. They did not fight in the large mass formation of the Gauls, the Germans, and the Romans themselves, but rather in small groups using guerrilla tactics, with scattered attacks and sharp, short, sudden sallies. Most dangerous of all was the use they made of chariots—small, two-wheeled battle carts drawn by fast horses—for the quick, stinging blow and the equally quick retreat. At one time, four thousand such chariots had taken the field against Caesar.

Caesar returned with a number of British slaves, but not much other booty. Some of Rome's citizens were disappointed with the meager results. "I hear there is no gold or silver in Britain," we read in a letter written shortly after Caesar's return. "And as far as the British people are concerned, I don't believe they will bring us either knowledge or entertainment." There was no profit

*He had learned that it would not be easy to conquer Britain.*

in the venture, and nearly a hundred years had to go by before Roman troops again crossed the Channel. But other men, among them the historian Plutarch, saw more than merely an unprofitable expedition. To them, the invasion of Britain was "the most famous testimony of Caesar's courage. He was the first who brought a navy into the Western ocean, or who sailed the Atlantic with an army to make war. It can be said that Caesar carried the Roman Empire beyond the limits of the known world."

Besides, Caesar had shown that he could cross the Channel at his pleasure. If any of the nations along the coast of Gaul still thought of revolt, they now knew that Britain would offer them no refuge from Caesar's punishment.

There were living in Gaul at that time nearly twenty million people. They were a spirited and gifted race. And yet, Caesar, with a force of never more than a hundred thousand legionnaires, was keeping the whole country in submission.

For the Gauls were ceaselessly fighting among themselves. Nation fought nation. Every tribe, every clan, indeed, every great household of Gaul stood divided against itself. Whenever Caesar marched against one of the nations, he could be sure that its jealous neighbors would rush to his aid. But what if they should ever join together in a common cause against him? What if they should combine to defy him under a single leader?

Such a leader at last arose. His name was Vercinget-orix, son of Celtillus. His father had once been the greatest man in the whole country, the chieftain of the whole of Gaul. But when he had attempted to make himself their king, the Gauls had slain him.

Vercingetorix could not forget his father's dream of a united Gaul. But the Gallic chiefs around him, among them his own uncle, would not hear of his plans, and finally drove the young prince from Gergovia, his native city. Homeless and stripped of his inheritance, the out-cast prince now roamed the land a soldier of fortune, seeking support among the discontent and uprooted—the "rabble," Caesar called them—that swarmed up and down the country. Vercingetorix now called on this "rabble" to rally in a common fight for freedom; and when at last he returned to Gergovia, he had recruited a large army filled with a fighting spirit far more formidable than any that had yet risen against Caesar. Vercingetorix now in his turn drove out the chiefs who had expelled him, was proclaimed king, and became supreme com-mander of the united Gallic armies.

The young king proved himself a master of or-ganization. Establishing an iron discipline—death for a serious crime, the loss of an ear or an eye for lesser offenses—and reducing Gallic methods of warfare to a system, he welded his unruly soldiers together in an efficient war machine. And the campaign plan that he had conceived and that he now began to execute shows how clearly he understood the difficulty of his self-chosen task.

All around the Mediterranean the Roman legions had taken country after country: but until Caesar took command they had avoided Gaul. Gallic forces had more than once defeated Roman troops led by one or the other of Caesar's lieutenants. Only when Caesar himself was in command were the Roman legions invincible.

It was the midst of winter. Caesar was in Italy, his Gallic legions in their winter camps in northern and central Gaul. He, Vercingetorix, would strike now: while snow and ice still covered the mountain passes, he would block Caesar's return to Gaul, throw his full force against each of the Roman garrisons, and crush them one by one. Cut off from their incomparable leader they would fall.

When Caesar at last heard of the plot, vast Gallic forces were gathering to fall upon the Roman legions in the center of Gaul. The Roman acted with lightning speed to meet the danger. He sent a small cavalry troop to the northern frontier of Provence, strengthened the stations along its western frontiers, and then, at the head of a small force, invaded southern Gaul. Crossing the Cévennes Mountains, here towering three thousand feet and higher, by passes that lay under six feet of snow and had never before been crossed in winter, he took by surprise the nations who had thought themselves safe. Caesar's cavalry burned, looted, and ravaged the undefended country and spread terror far and wide.

The news of the invasion quickly reached Vercingetorix. He knew that he must go at once to defend the invaded nations; for if he failed them now, his great alliance would fall apart. He turned his armies south, and marched to meet Caesar.

But Caesar, two days after he had come, turned his command over to Decimus Brutus, instructing him to scorch the earth as far as his troops could reach. Then Caesar slipped away. Not even Brutus, not even his own small escort knew his destination.

Caesar sped to the northern border of Provence. Here he picked up the cavalry he had sent earlier, and at their head rode day and night without a halt through two hundred miles of snow and slush and the roadless forests of enemy country, until his steaming horses reached the winter camp of two legions quartered in northern Gaul. Fresh riders swarmed out minutes later to all the other Roman camps scattered over Gaul, to call the Roman armies together. Within days, Caesar accomplished what Vercingetorix had dreaded most: the Roman general stood in the very heart of Gaul surrounded by ten splendid legions.

As the two great opponents faced each other, they

both knew now what was the greatest weakness of the Roman, the greatest strength of the Gaul. Caesar was fighting in enemy country, Vercingetorix on home ground.

In open battle, Caesar had never been beaten. But fight or not, his legions must have food, his horses fodder. If Gallic swords had not defeated Caesar, the king of Gaul decided, hunger would conquer him.

# THE GREAT SIEGE

## Chapter Nine

THUS, EARLY IN THE SPRING OF 52 B.C., began the war that, in Caesar's words, "was different from all other wars."

The fields were bare. There was no grass to cut. The Gauls around the Roman winter camps who were to bring in grain and fodder had vanished. The Roman parties that ventured from the camps to forage for food, or to bring in timber, returned bloody and empty-handed, for thousands upon thousands of Gallic horsemen swarmed the country, or prowled about the forests nearby to fall upon the Roman detachments, shower them with javelins and arrows, and be gone before the legionnaires could strike back.

Meanwhile, the main body of the Gallic army—more than eighty thousand foot soldiers—kept at a safe distance. They destroyed the bridges in Caesar's path over rivers swelled with the spring thaw. They kept a close watch on the borders of Provence, and blocked supplies, fresh troops, fresh horses from reaching Caesar. And they scorched the earth before him. The barns and farms and villages and towns toward which Caesar turned in search of grain and fodder went up in flames at his approach. His legionnaires soon felt the pinch of hunger.

The Gauls whose homes were set afire at their king's command consoled themselves that the flames were torches of freedom. But there was one city in all of Gaul which they could not find it in their hearts to sacrifice, the city of Avaricum, today called Bourges. Vercingetorix demanded that it, too, be razed—but his chiefs would not have it so. It was the most beautiful city in all the country, they said, and so well defended by nature with marsh and hills and rivers all around that even Caesar could not capture it.

They did not know even yet what Caesar and his men were made of. Although the legions were weak with hunger, they marched upon the city. After a furious siege that lasted for a month, the Romans took Avaricum in a fierce assault. The struggle had been bitter, and it ended in slaughter: of forty thousand Gauls who had defended Avaricum, less than eight hundred survived the city's fall.

Vast stores of grain and all kinds of supplies fell to the

Romans. With food once more secure, Caesar gave his legions a well-earned rest.

But he himself was restless. "Winter was almost over," he writes, "the time was ripe for military operations." He craved the final test of strength, the battle of decision against Vercingetorix. But the Gaul refused to meet head-on the legions under Caesar's command. Until their strength was broken by hunger, he would not give battle.

For months now, Vercingetorix had had his way—he had resisted and outmaneuvered one of the greatest generals the world has known. If any of the Gallic nations had so far remained neutral, in fear of Roman victory, they now threw in their lot with Vercingetorix. Caesar, surrounded by a country in revolt, like a ship that is threatened on all sides by an angry sea, decided first of all to restore contact with Roman territory. Reluctantly, he turned his forces toward Provence.

It was a bitter moment for him. The labor of years spent in the conquest of Gaul seemed lost.

But to the Gauls united under Vercingetorix it was the hour of triumph. The Gallic king called together all his commanders and spoke to them proudly:

"The Roman legions have turned tail, and are on the run back to their Provence. We have won back our freedom. But there is one thing more for us to do. We must now destroy the Romans completely, or else they will return with fresh and larger armies, and go on making war on us. This is the moment to deal them the final blow. We shall strike while they are on the retreat and overburdened with the baggage they are carrying."

Filled with a fighting spirit that comes from the certainty of victory, the whole Gallic army threw itself into Caesar's path. The Roman marching columns, emerging from a valley near Dijon into the plain beyond, found their road ahead blocked by five thousand Gallic horsemen. And on the hills to their left, and the hills to their right, two other cavalry armies, each of the same size, were closing in. Eighty thousand foot soldiers hovered in the distance.

Caesar was taken by surprise—he had expected no attack. All he had to oppose a cavalry charge were five thousand riders at the most, among them a thousand German mercenaries he had called from across the Rhine. But he at once drew up his forces in battle order, seized the attack, and scattered the whole host of Gallic horsemen. His riders gave pursuit and a great slaughter followed. Thousand of Gauls died with their mounts in that battle; and where it took place, French peasants may still on occasion find a Gallic horseshoe in their fields.

No sooner were the Gallic horsemen scattered or destroyed than Caesar dropped all thought of retreat. He turned upon the Gallic foot army to fight at last the decisive battle. But his opponent knew that his eighty thousand Gauls were not a match for Caesar with ten legions. He abandoned his camp, and hurriedly withdrew with all his forces into the nearby mountain fortress of Alesia. He sent his cavalry—or what was left of it—away to ride through the width and length of Gaul and summon help. Then the gates of the fortress slammed shut, and Alesia prepared to defend itself until relief came. Caesar's great challenger was at bay.

In later days, when the men of Rome recalled the events that took place at Alesia, they used to say that no mortal man could plan what Caesar planned, and only a god could do what Caesar did.

The stronghold of Alesia stood high on a hill in the mountainous country of central Gaul, near where today nestles the town of Alise-Sainte-Reine. The hill itself is overtopped by a large, flat plateau or table of solid rock, with a sheer drop all around, half a mile wide and more than a mile long, which towers five hundred feet above the surrounding valleys. In three directions—to the north, the east, and the south—rivers and more hills enclose the rock-crowned eminence with a natural bulwark shaped like a vast horseshoe. Only toward the west, the slope below the rock descends gradually into a plain three miles in width which forms the open end of the great horseshoe. To these formidable defenses raised by nature the Gauls had added miles of walls and trenches, to make the stronghold still stronger.

Inside that fortress there were now eighty thousand of Gaul's finest fighters, commanded by their great king. Outside, beyond the hilltops in every direction, the nations of Gaul were gathering together all their armed men to march and ride to the king's aid.

Caesar slowly rode around the mighty enclosure. When he completed the circle, he knew that he could not take Alesia by storm. He gave orders, and his legionnaires went to work.

First, they closed the open end of the horseshoe with a trench three miles long and twenty feet wide, its sides cutting straight down twenty feet into the rocky soil. Around the rest of the circle, eight fortified camps rose up to stand guard. This was Caesar's first line of defense, enough to keep the enemy from attempting a mass escape at night, and from harassing his soldiers who only now began to build the real siege works.

Six to eight hundred feet back of the first great trench, well out of javelin range, and then all around the fortress, they cut two more trenches, each fifteen feet in depth, one filled with water from the rivers. Behind these, they raised an unbroken wall of palisades, a full ten miles all around, topped along their entire length with breastworks and battlements, studded with towers from which stones, javelins, and arrows could be cast down upon an assailant, and bristling with sharpened branches, "like stags' horns," through which no man could scale the wall. This ring tied together the eight camps. The Roman troops could now be shifted freely to any point without fear of being cut off by the forces in Alesia.

But Caesar knew that he had to reckon with another force as well—the Gallic army of relief that was even now on the way to free Vercingetorix from Caesar's stranglehold. They, too, would find him prepared. He built another ring of fortifications like the first, but facing outward, and thirteen miles in length. Nor did he rest there.

Caesar had with him at Alesia eleven legions—some fifty thousand Roman soldiers; about five thousand horsemen, including the thousand German mercenaries; and some twenty thousand light troops—slingers, and archers—from the islands of the Mediterranean Sea and from Numidia. This force would have to man the inner circle of ten miles, the outer circle of thirteen miles, and guard its entire length against the forces of all Gaul. "I decided to fortify still more," he writes, "so that my lines could be held at any point by a small number of men."

The work went on. Inside and outside the great circle, beyond the big trenches, he set five rows of shallow ditches studded with sharpened branches that threatened death to a charging enemy. His soldiers called them tombstones. Beyond the tombstones were eight rows of round, shallow pits set out in checkerboard fashion, with stakes as thick as a man's thigh raising their sharp, fire-hardened points straight upward under a concealing cover of twigs. "Lillies," said his soldiers. Beyond them still were row upon row of wooden blocks with iron hooks embedded just below the surface of the ground to trap attackers—"spurs" in the slang of Caesar's men.

Caesar's legions worked with unstinting ardor and devotion. "I could have overturned the heavens with these men," Caesar later told the Roman people. In forty days, the bristling double wall around Alesia was completed. It was not a day too soon.

Meanwhile, the Gauls inside the beleaguered city were growing desperate. Their food, even though it had been rationed carefully since the first days of the siege, was running out. One of the chiefs even stood up in council to urge that the soldiers should keep up their strength by killing and eating those of the townspeople too old, too young, or too weak to fight. Mercifully, his advice was not followed—but the besieged army drove the old men, the women, and the children out of the gates toward the Roman lines. They made their way to the Roman battlements to beg for food, and to offer themselves as slaves. The Romans drove them back into the fortress.

And then, two days after Caesar had finished his fortifications, the armies of Gaul were upon him. Two hundred and fifty thousand fighters from all Gallic nations, commanded by the Gaul Commius, had come to crush Caesar. As they drew up a mile from Caesar's lines, their cavalry alone covered the three-mile plain.

On the first day of battle, Commius relied almost entirely on his great host of horsemen, among whom he had scattered archers and slingers. They outnumbered Caesar's cavalry three or four to one. The mounted battle raged from noon until sunset—but finally Caesar's men broke the attack. Commius' riders turned and scattered, and the pursuing Roman forces slew many of the slingers and archers who could not flee as fast. When Vercingetorix and his men, who watched the action from the slopes inside, saw their comrades driven from the field, they withdrew sadly into their fortress. "They had almost given up hope," Caesar writes.

In this first bloody encounter, the Gauls had come up against Caesar's formidable barriers. They now set themselves to making hurdles, scaling ladders, grappling hooks, mantlets, poles, and other equipment with which to overcome the Roman defenses. Thus the next day passed quietly, with only scattered skirmishes now and then. But in the midst of the following night, the legionnaires up on the ramparts leaped to their arms as a vast Gallic force flooded up against their outer defenses, hailing clouds of stones and arrows and javelins down on the defenders. At the same moment, Alesia's garrison broke from the gates. But in the dark of night, the trenches, pits and traps and hooks took their toll. At dawn, Commius' force had failed to breach the Roman lines at any point, and Vercingetorix's troops had not even come close to the main defenses.

Defeated for a second time, the Gauls withdrew. Another day passed quietly, while both sides girded themselves for the supreme test.

The scouts of Commius had searched and probed all along the Roman line of defense to find a weak spot. At last they discovered a stretch in the fortifications that was less well defended than the rest. A hill too wide to be enclosed within the circle had forced Caesar to set one of his camps up on a slope that was not a favorable place for the Roman forces.

Here Commius would strike. From among his troops he picked a task force of the best fighters—sixty-five thousand of them, a force larger than all of Caesar's legions put together. Under cover of darkness, they moved within striking distance of the chosen spot, concealed themselves and their heavy equipment behind a hill, and rested until the sun was high in the sky.

At midday, the storm of battle broke in all its fury. The Gallic trumpets called to the attack, the battle cries of all the nations of Gaul answered and echoed from hill to hill. From the heights above Caesar's weakest camp, the great task force poured down, threw its scaling ladders and hurdles across the spurs, the lillies, and the tomb-stones, and passed over them to scale the ramparts of the camp itself. At the same time, Commius' other forces swarmed all around the vast circle, threatening now here, now there, so that the Romans could not leave a single sector of their thirteen-mile palisades unguarded for a moment. From inside the fortress of Alesia, Vercinget-orix's army sallied forth to the attack. Watching the action from the walls of Alesia, Vercingetorix at once understood Commius' plan, and threw his main force into the same stretch which Commius' task force was storming from without. At this one point alone, Caesar's men stood up to armies twice the size of their entire force.

The battle of Alesia that day surpasses the imagina-tion. A ring of Romans ten miles long and more, and facing in both directions, was fighting back to back against a raging nation. From a look-out commanding a view of every sector of the roaring battle, Caesar led the action. He wore the scarlet robe by which friend and foe knew him.

His own description of the battle hardly mentions the extreme danger in which he found himself that day. His thoughts are with his legionnaires:

"My men, strung out along the whole length of the fortifications, did not find it easy to beat off the attacks coming from every side. Besides, they were much troubled by the noise of battle coming from behind their backs. They realized that their lives depended not just on their own courage, but on the courage of those who were fighting back to back with them. And men are as a rule more fearful of a danger which they cannot see than of a danger that is before their eyes."

But every Gaul and every Roman knew that everything depended on this struggle, and so they fought as they had never fought before. "The Gauls," says Caesar, "saw that all was lost if they could not break through our lines. The Romans knew that if they just stood firm today all their hardship would be ended."

Twice Caesar himself joined in the fighting, taking command at points where disaster threatened. He had sent one of his best lieutenants, Labienus, to direct the defense against Commius' task force. Now Labienus sent a message of distress. His legionnaires could not hold out much longer at the point against which Commius had thrown his strongest units. Under the cover of their interlocking shields—the famous tortoise formation—the Gauls had covered up the lines of traps, filled in the trenches, heaped ramps of earth against the palisades, and were about to spill over the ramparts. The Romans were running short of javelins and arrows and their strength was ebbing, while the Gauls were constantly moving fresh men up into the fighting. He,

Labienus, would have to surrender the position and with his men fight his way out.

Caesar hastily scraped together a handful of troops from less exposed sectors of the line, and went to join Labienus at the moment of his greatest danger. At the approach of their great general, new courage ran through the legionnaires. They dropped their bows, forgot their javelins, and drew their swords to throw themselves upon the Gauls.

Under this fierce assault, the Gallic task force cracked. The soldiers of Commius, who only a moment ago had pressed forward, now turned and ran. Caesar's cavalry at once gave chase and slew them as they fled.

This rout of their best men, which could be seen from all the hill slopes around, drained the whole Gallic host of its fighting spirit. Inside the Roman ring, Vercingetorix and his troops withdrew into the fortress of Alesia in despair. Outside, the great army of Commius fell apart; they gave up fighting and fled to the various nations from where they had come. In Plutarch's words, "so vast an army vanished like a ghost, or a dream."

Up in the fortress of Alesia, the king addressed his chiefs. "I have fought," he said, "not for myself but for the freedom of us all. I am defeated. I place myself into your hands, to do with me as you think best. You may kill me, and so win Caesar's favor. Or, you may give me up to him alive."

*Then Vercingetorix sat down at Caesar's feet.*

Other writers than Caesar recorded the scene which ended the great and last revolt of the Gauls. Hirtius wrote:

"Then Vercingetorix, who was the chief spring of all the war, put on his finest armor, and his richest robes. On his horse covered with the richest caparison, he rode out of the gates of Alesia toward Caesar, who was seated in a chair of state. Once around Caesar he rode, in silence. Then he descended from his horse, took off his robes and armor, and laid them on the ground, and himself went and sat down at Caesar's feet and never said a word. Then he was led away."

All Gaul lay conquered. Caesar could make peace, and he made it on terms so wise and generous that the Gallic nations remained loyal to him through all the trying years that followed. Soon a full legion made up of Gallic fighters served gallantly under his standards. From the birds' wings with which the Gallic soldiers adorned their Roman helmets, their legion became known as The Crested Lark.

# CAESAR AND POMPEY

## Chapter Ten

LANDS TWICE AS LARGE AS ALL of Italy—a people richer and more numerous than that of Spain: these were the gifts that Caesar brought to Rome with his conquest of Gaul. Late in the year 50 B.C. he returned to Italy in expectation of his just reward.

But through the years that Caesar had spent fighting abroad, the government of Rome had once more drifted into chaos. Of the two men who nine years earlier had joined hands with Caesar to set the state in order, one was dead: Crassus had lost his life in battle in the eastern provinces. The other, general Pompey the Great, had not known how to rule. Left to its own devices, the Roman Senate lost itself in a mad scramble for offices and wealth. While Caesar's legionnaires were bleeding in their battle to the death with Vercingetorix, lawlessness reached such a height in the city of Rome that the Senate, frightened at last, proclaimed martial law. It called on Pompey to put troops on foot in Italy, and to restore at least an outward order. Under a new title—sole consul—Pompey now held in his hands the supreme power of the empire. His soldiers everywhere made clear beyond a doubt that Pompey was master.

There was then in all of Rome only one man great enough to stand by Pompey's side, and that was Caesar, conqueror of Gaul. But Pompey was no longer willing to share the rule with Caesar, as he had done while Crassus was alive. Was it the sweet taste of unlimited power that now moved Pompey? We shall never know with certainty. But we do know precisely what was decided that day in Rome at Pompey's bidding: it was that Caesar, the victor of Alesia, must be destroyed.

On January 7, 49 B.C., the Roman Senate ordered Caesar to strip himself of his command, his office, and his legions—on pain of being declared a public enemy. They knew in Rome, as they had learned abroad, that Caesar with his legions was invincible. But if he could be brought to send his men away, his enemies could deal with him at their pleasure.

Caesar was wintering then with one legion in Ravenna, a coastal city in his north Italian province. The bitter news reached him on January 10, through friends who had escaped from Rome in terror of their lives.

Would Caesar obey? He knew full well that once he was defenseless, his enemies would take his life or drive him from the country—and Rome, the Empire which he had served so well, would be, as Plutarch put it, "left to be tossed about like a ship adrift without a pilot." Or should he defy Pompey while he was still strong? That would mean civil war—and he, Caesar, an outlaw. They say that Caesar wavered for an hour. Then he made up his mind.

A few miles south of Ravenna, a little stream, then called the Rubicon, flows eastward into the nearby Adriatic Sea. It marked the border between Caesar's province and the Roman homelands. Like Romulus' sacred furrow, to cross it under arms was to break the peace of Rome.

On January 12, Caesar ordered his legionnaires across. "The die is cast," he said—there was no turning back. The news flew to Rome, through Italy, through all the empire: Caesar has crossed the Rubicon! It's civil war!

The revolutionary army with which Caesar invaded Roman soil consisted of the single legion that he had with him at Ravenna. His other troops, called from their winter camps in Gaul, would not arrive for weeks. Pompey had to oppose him the full might of Rome—ten legions standing under arms in Italy alone. Yet Caesar marched ahead—and Pompey hastily left Rome and, in the company of many of the Senators and noblemen, withdrew his forces to the south.

Caesar marched on. While Pompey and his followers now spoke of him as The Monster, town after town in his path threw open its gates to welcome him. Swarms of legionnaires left Pompey's standards to serve Caesar. Three Pompeian legions, cut off at Corfinium, surrendered to him without a blow. Pompey, left now with only five legions, fled on to Brindisi, the Adriatic seaport nearest the coast of Greece. He rounded up every galley and transport ship from the ports up and down the coast, and with his whole force escaped across the water to the Greek port of Durazzo. Ten weeks after crossing the Rubicon, Caesar, without bloodshed, was master of all Italy.

"My way of conquest will be of a new kind," Caesar wrote at that time in a letter to two of his friends. "I shall gain my strength by being understanding, and generous." He kept his word. The officers of Pompey who now fell into his hands were sent away in peace and safety; and his march into Rome after Pompey's escape saw none of the horrors of bloodshed and revenge that had marked the struggle between Marius and Sulla. It was soon said with admiration that Caesar was incapable of holding grudges, and willing at the least chance to make peace with his bitterest enemies.

After Ravenna, Caesar kept sending message after message to Pompey offering peace. Pompey refused to listen. In Rome now, Caesar called together the Senators who had remained in the city, and urged them to send yet another peace mission to the general. The Senators were favorable to the proposal—but not one among them could be found to carry the message to Durazzo. They were afraid, every one of them, to place their lives in Pompey's power.

Although Caesar now held all of Italy, Pompey's great armies lay around him like pincers. In the east, the general was collecting vast forces on Greek soil to invade Italy. And in the west, seven of Pompey's strongest legions, commanded by his ablest leaders, were threatening from Spain.

Caesar decided to deal first with the greater danger. After three days in Rome, he set out for Spain. "I am going now to meet an army without a general," he quipped, "when I come back I shall go to meet a general without an army."

He took to Spain six legions, against Pompey's seven. Once there, he hounded and harassed and outmaneuvered his opponents, courted disaster in his rapid marches to cut their supplies, and even changed the course of a river to gain a mere advantage of position. But when at last he had them at his mercy, when all his men and officers were clamoring for battle and for glory, when victory was within his grasp—Caesar refused to strike.

"My soldiers were saying it out in the open that I was just throwing away a splendid chance of victory—and for that, they said, they would not fight for me next time I asked them," he writes. "But a good general should win his victories not just by force, but also by intelligence." So the boldest of generals held back his battle-eager legions, and waited.

Within a few days events proved him right: Pompey's main Spanish force laid down its arms before him without another blow. It was a stunning victory, all the more brilliant as its cost in blood had been so low. Caesar discharged Pompey's officers, paid off the legionnaires, and issued food to all. Then he returned to Rome, after an absence of only forty days. But now the western part of Rome's empire was under his command.

To the east, across the sea in Greece, Pompey had not been idle. He could now put in the field nine Roman legions, three thousand archers, more than a thousand slingers, and seven thousand cavalry. Two more legions were on their way from Asia to join him. As soon as winter ended, he planned to return to Italy and recapture Rome.

But Caesar did not intend to let his rival choose the time or place of battle. It was mid-winter, and the seas were rough. The Pompeian navy, five hundred ships in all, patrolled the seaways. Yet Caesar slipped across. On January 4, 48 B.C., he sailed from Brindisi with half his force—fifteen thousand legionnaires, five hundred horsemen—and landed safely on a deserted stretch of the rocky coast south of Durazzo. Three months were to go by before the rest of his army could follow.

The two great rivals stood face to face. At stake was the Roman Empire. Rarely in history have the prizes of war been higher—and rarely has there been a stranger war than that which now began among the craggy mountains of the Greek peninsula.

The troops commanded by Pompey outnumbered his opponent's. The seas were under his command, and with them all the foodstuffs, gold, and war supplies from Egypt, Africa, and the East. His warehouses in Durazzo bulged with materials of all kinds gathered through the year. His troops, well fed, well armed, and well rested, were at their fighting peak.

Against him, Caesar could put in the field only one legionnaire for every two, only one man on horseback for every seven. His men had made an arduous march the length and breadth of Spain and Italy, and crossed a stormy sea. He carried no supplies, and had no fleet to get them, but had to live off the country where he fought. In fact, there came a moment when Caesar's troops were faced with naked hunger. But they did not lose heart. From grass and roots and tree bark they ground a meal to keep their stomachs filled. "I am fighting against wild beasts!" Pompey cried when he first saw a piece of their strange food.

And yet—of the two rivals matched so unevenly— it was always Caesar, Caesar not Pompey, who was on the attack. Day after day Caesar offered battle, and day after day, month after month, Pompey refused to fight.

Once only in that war did Pompey's forces dare an offensive; it was when Caesar's men had thrown fortifications around Pompey's host, blockading it against the coast line of Durazzo Bay. Before the trap had been quite closed, two Gallic noblemen in Caesar's camp, the brothers Egus and Rancillus, turned traitors and informed Pompey of the weak spot in Caesar's line. This once, Pompey struck—and broke the blockade.

Pompey, it seems, was well content with his success that day. Not so Caesar. The day was still young—it was barely noon. Caesar rode quickly to the scene, regrouped his troops, and led a furious counterattack. The battle was hot: one hundred thirty thousand arrows lay scattered on the field when it was over. But for the second time that day luck was against Caesar. He was repulsed, and nearly lost his life.

"If Pompey only knew how to win a victory," Caesar said when night fell, "he could have taken me today."

Now that his blockade was broken and therefore useless, Caesar moved on, marching soon after sunset on the very day of battle. He was hoping to draw his enemy after him, into a territory where he could force battle. He found the setting that he needed on the plain of Pharsalus, along the banks of the Enipeus River, and set up camp there. Pompey soon caught up with him and encamped up on a hilltop some three miles away.

Day after day, Caesar drew up his forces on the plain, a little nearer to Pompey's camp each time, and invited battle. Again, Pompey stalled—he kept his men high on the hill slope, under the very ramparts of his camp, to which they could withdraw if Caesar should attack. The world of Rome stood breathless, awaiting who would win the greatest prize on earth. But Pompey could not bring himself to fight it out.

There were in Pompey's camp men as heartily tired of the delay as Caesar himself: the Senators, the noblemen, the men of rank and fashion who had come along from Rome with Pompey. Seeing around them daily the vast host of Pompey's army, they had no doubt that victory was his for the taking. "Why delay," they urged the general, "why not crush Caesar now? Then we can all go back to Rome, drive Caesar's followers from their splendid houses, and enjoy the spoils of victory!" So sure they were of winning that they fell to quarreling among themselves over the wealth, the offices of state, and the posts of honor which they thought would soon be theirs.

Pompey delayed. Weeks passed, and still Pompey would not give battle. Caesar decided that he must once more change his tactics. He would move on and keep moving, in hopes of luring Pompey to a spot where battle could no longer be refused. On August 9, he gave the orders to break camp and march.

The tents were struck, the camp walls leveled, and his

men were forming in their marching columns when Caesar saw that this day Pompey, yielding at last to the demands of his companions, had moved his lines a little farther down the slopes than usual, to a position where they could be engaged on even terms. At once he hoisted the red flag of battle and summoned his commanders.

"We must put off our travels for the moment," he said, "and think of battle—the battle for which we have hoped so long."

The trumpets sounded. Eagerly the legionnaires dropped their marching bundles and found their ranks. As they marched past him to the field, Caesar hailed one of his captains, a veteran of many years and many battles.

"Crastinus," he called out, "tell me—what do you think this day will bring for us?"

"Victory, my commander!" Crastinus called back. "And if I live or if I die, today I will give you reason to be proud of me."

The ranks of Pompey's fifty thousand legionnaires stretched across the plain of Pharsalus, from the steep bank of the Enipeus River on their right up to the foot-hills on the left. There on the hills Pompey massed his seven thousand cavalry. With them he meant to overpower Caesar's right wing, outflank his legions, and crush them as if in a vise.

Caesar's legions, only twenty thousand strong, were strung out across the plain to match the length of Pompey's front. Both armies, as usual, drew up three lines deep.

Caesar, meanwhile, had studied the grouping of Pompey's forces. He now picked out of his third line a crack force for a special task. He gave them their instructions and formed them in a fourth line on his right wing, behind the small cavalry troop he could throw against Pompey's seven thousand riders. Caesar himself, as was his custom, took his command post with his right wing.

Now the watchword was passed through Caesar's ranks: "Venus Victorious!" Then Caesar's bugles sounded the attack.

His legions moved forward into the no-man's-land— a thousand feet wide—that lay between them and the enemy. At first they advanced slowly, then faster and faster—until they broke into a run to meet the charge of Pompey's men.

Pompey's ranks did not stir. They had been ordered to stand their ground and await the onslaught where they had been placed; for Pompey thought that in this manner Caesar's men would arrive breathless, and weakened by the doubly long uphill race. But Caesar's men were seasoned fighters, with the experience of many battles, and so Pompey's ruse failed. All of their own accord, the twenty thousand legionnaires of Caesar stopped halfway to regain their breath. Now they charged again —a single volley of javelins flew before them—they drew their swords, and now they were upon the enemy. The roaring lines swayed back and forth in furious fighting. Romans were fighting Romans, and neither side would yield.

At the precise moment when legion crashed against legion, Pompey's massed horsemen charged forward to take Caesar's right flank. They came swarming down the hills, and the outcome could not be in doubt: Caesar's small force of riders, outnumbered seven to one, was steadily pressed back. Pompey's cavalry forced its way behind Caesar's lines and began to wheel off to strike the legions in the back.

This was Caesar's moment. He raised his hand. His short fourth rank of crack troops, standing by idly until now, suddenly charged into action. They rushed toward Pompey's riders at a furious run, swords by their sides, their javelins ready in their hands. Stunned by the suddenness of the attack, the Pompeian horsemen drew in their reins and braced themselves against the hail of javelins that must now come flying.

But no javelins flew. Caesar's legionnaires, true to their orders, raced right up to the horses, javelins in hand —and now they struck and jabbed and slashed with their long pointed weapons, not at the horses but at the eyes and faces of the mounted men.

This unexpected, frightening assault, delivered with a will, threw Pompey's young, unseasoned riders into

*And now they struck at the eyes and faces of the mounted men.*

complete confusion. In fear, they tried to protect their faces—unseeing, they could not stand their ground. Their ranks crumbled, they turned about, and fled. Pompey's proud cavalry, on which he had staked the battle, was scattered.

Caesar's crack force did not pause here. Their charge had carried them across the line of battle, and into the flank of Pompey's force. Another signal—and Caesar's first and second lines, who had engaged the enemy along the entire front, opened their ranks and fell back to let the third line move into the fighting. Pompey's legions, set upon by fresh troops, stripped of the cover of their cavalry, and outflanked in their turn, were steadily pressed back.

"When Pompey saw his cavalry so broken up and in full flight," Plutarch writes, "he knew himself no longer. He rushed back to his camp like a man who has lost his mind, sat down inside his tent, and waited for come what may. When some of Caesar's soldiers burst into the camp soon afterward, he only said: 'What—even into my camp?' Then he threw off his general's robe, put on simple garments, and leaped upon his horse and fled."

It was all over. In one pitched battle, which may have lasted little longer than an hour, Caesar defeated an army more than twice the size of his own forces.

And even in this moment of his triumph, Caesar did not forget that those who stood against him were Romans like himself. "Spare your fellow Romans!" he shouted to his men who pressed forward in pursuit. The Romans of Pompey's army were quick to understand. "Stand and fear not!" the call went out among them. They stood, lowered their swords—and so saved their lives, while Caesar's men charged past them, leaving them unharmed.

And yet, much Roman blood was spilled that day. Of Caesar's men twelve hundred lost their lives, of Pompey's six thousand. As Caesar rode past the bodies of his dead enemies he pondered how he had offered peace to Pompey not less than seven times since he had marched across the Rubicon, and how he had as often been refused.

"They brought it on themselves," he said. "They would have put me to death——me, Caesar, in spite of all my victories——if I had not called on my legions to support me."

Then he sent his men to seek out the dead body of Crastinus, his captain who had led the charge that turned the battle, and buried him with military honors.

# RULER OF ROME

## Chapter Eleven

THE STORY GOES THAT AT THE very hour when Caesar's legions burst into Pompey's camp at Pharsalus, a palm tree shot out of the ground in Tralles, in far-off Asia, and spread its crown over a bust of Caesar that stood there in the Temple of Victory. And back in Italy, a Paduan priest who had been watching sacred signs cried out at the same moment, "Caesar—you are the victor!"

This legend, like many others, is only a truth in disguise: the tremendous news of Pharsalus traveled with lightning speed to every corner of the empire—and where it went men understood that Caesar on that day had won more than one battle—Caesar had won the war.

But Pompey's followers were not yet ready to accept defeat. They met, and swore to fight on. Just one among them, famous Cicero, now raised his voice to urge peace with Caesar. He nearly lost his life for it.

Pompey himself, meanwhile, fled to a Greek seaport, took a ship, and set his sails for Egypt. With only a handful of troops Caesar followed by land and sea. He meant no harm to his defeated rival—only to face him at last and compel him to make peace. But when Caesar arrived, late in September, in Alexandria, messengers from the Egyptian court received him with a fearful welcome present: the bloody head of Pompey, chopped from its body by the court's hired killers, and Pompey's signet ring.

Caesar in silence took the ring and gazed upon its mark which he knew so well—a lion, holding a sword. He would not look at Pompey's head—instead, he raised his cloak, covered his face, and wept deeply that so great a Roman had lost his life in a tragic and unworthy manner.

Swift couriers raced to Rome with the news of the general's death. The Roman street crowds, eager to turn upon the memory of the man who had been their master, threw Pompey's marble bust down from its place of honor and smashed it to the ground.

In Egypt, Caesar was delayed. A young prince and his sister were quarreling over the country's crown, and Caesar, Roman consul, thought it his duty to settle their dispute. But the wintry season slowed down the arrival of fresh troops, and so it was March of the next year (47 B.C.) before he could make himself master of Egypt. He gave the throne to Princess Cleopatra together with her younger brother. At last he set out for home, marching along Rome's eastern provinces and tending to the business of the empire. Near Zela, he came upon the king of Parthia with an invading army. Caesar attacked, and destroyed the enemy in a battle that lasted little longer than it takes to read Caesar's report of it: "I came, saw, conquered."

At the end of September, he was back in Rome. A year and more had passed since Caesar scattered Pompey's legions at Pharsalus. During that time, Pompey's two sons had raised another army in Africa, in the vain hope that they could wrest the empire from Caesar's hands. Their folly compelled him to break off his work of peace in Rome after a short three months, and go to war against them. He sailed for Africa on December 27.

The armies of Pompey's sons, and of their African ally King Juba, were quickly crushed by Caesar's generalship, shown here at its most brilliant. It was in this campaign that Caesar's legionnaires for the first time met African fighting elephants, and easily learned to deal with the huge animals whom they contemptuously called "Juba's cows." Their leader conquered for the empire a new province in Africa, which from now on would send to Rome vast quantities of grain and oil each year. Caesar returned to Rome in triumph.

Caesar had meant to disband his old legions now. But there was not yet to be peace. The sons of Pompey, who had escaped to Spain from Africa, were threatening again with a new army, thirteen legions strong. Once more, Caesar marched. He went to Spain with eight legions to fight it out with Pompey's sons. For weeks and weeks they slipped away from him, avoiding battle until he nearly drove them off the map. At last they had to make a stand—deep in the south of Spain, near the town of Munda. There, on March 17, 45 B.C., Caesar destroyed them. It was his last and nearly his bloodiest battle. Thirty thousand Pompeians lost their lives that day. The final blaze of civil war was quenched in a stream of blood.

Caesar at last could turn his hand to the great work for which his whole life had been preparation: the reform of an empire in chaos. Sword in hand, he had crossed the Roman lands from one end to the other—and he had come to see, more clearly than any other man alive, that this great empire could not be held together with the sword alone. Something more was needed—something that neither Senate nor Pompey had brought to Rome: a government of justice, law, and order.

More urgently than he had ever done since the beginning of the civil war, Caesar now called on his former enemies to forget the past, and to join hands with him in the great reform. He quickly raised to posts of trust and honor many an able Roman who had fought against him only yesterday. At his command, the marble bust of Pompey was repaired, and now it stood again in its proud place, before the theater which Pompey had built as a gift to the people of Rome.

At last Caesar could pay off his old legionnaires, with money and with farms. Land was also distributed among the poor of Rome: one hundred thousand Romans received homesteads from Caesar's hands. He drafted plans to drain large marshes south of Rome and turn them into farmland, and meantime he cut back the use of slaves in Italy, so that the Roman farmer could find work more readily. Out in the provinces, he lightened the tax burden, and dealt out drastic punishment to any Roman governor who misused his power abroad. He laid the plans for new Roman cities in Africa and Greece, and for a canal through the neck of land at Corinth to shorten the sea route to the east. The city of Rome was to have a new, large seaport where ships from every corner of the world could put in safely. And there were plans for Rome's first public library.

Caesar would coordinate Rome's scattered laws, so that there might be equal justice and order in all the city's far-flung dealings. To the same end, he reformed the Roman calendar. Compared with vast campaigns, splendid public buildings, and great works to change the course of river or sea, a change in the way time is measured seems a small thing—indeed, many Romans of his day laughed at Caesar's calendar reform. And yet, of all of Caesar's works, this one proved the most lasting. To this day, the nations of the world count hours, days, and months, work and rest, plow, plant, and reap, by Caesar's calendar, which in two thousand years has needed only a single, small correction.

He worked with furious, untiring energy, and with a quickness of decision which made "Caesar's speed" a Roman byword. The work which he performed in the few months of 46 and 45 B.C. that he could spend in the city meant more to Rome and her dominions than all the laws since Sulla put together.

But Caesar worked alone. He held and used Rome's power singlehanded, and this his enemies would not forgive him. Caesar ruled alone—would he not in the end claim that all Rome was his, and make himself their king? True, a king's crown had just been offered him by one of his supporters, and Caesar had refused it with the words: "I am not king—I am Caesar!" But the proud Roman noblemen were not reassured. Like Sulla many years ago, they thought Caesar six times as dangerous as any other man.

Soon ugly rumors drifted through the city—of men meeting in secret and whispering of murder. His friends brought Caesar warning, and pleaded with him to be careful of his life. In reply, Caesar disbanded the Spanish bodyguard that used to escort him with naked swords, and went about in public unprotected. "My life is more important to Rome than it is to me," he said. In all his fearless years, he had never had less time to think of his own safety. For one great, self-set task still lay ahead.

There was then in the natural defenses of the Roman empire still one great and dangerous gap. True, the Atlantic Ocean and the Channel gave safety toward the west. Against the barbarians of the north stood the mighty barriers of the Rhine, the Alps, and the Black Sea. In the south, Rome held sway over the African coast from the Pillars of Hercules—today's Gibraltar—to the Nile. But between the Nile and the Black Sea, Rome's eastern frontiers lay open to the attack of the powerful and restless Parthians. The eastern provinces could be secured only by pushing Rome's dominion forward to the great natural barrier of the Euphrates valley.

In the first days of 44 B.C., Caesar made known his plan to set out on a great eastern campaign to buttress the empire against the Parthians. He would be gone for three years, he announced. Word went out to the legionnaires to prepare themselves and to meet in Rome at the end of winter, in mid-March.

If there were men in Rome who meant to strike down Caesar, they must strike now. For once his legions were gathered around their general, their swords and their devotion would place him beyond the reach of even the boldest assassin. Caesar's decision to make war on Parthia forced his enemies' hands.

The plot to murder Caesar sprang from the head of

Cassius, a splendid soldier of a noble family. He had served Pompey through the civil war, but Caesar had long since forgotten the matter, raised him to public office, and counted him his friend.

Another man whom Caesar thought his friend now joined in Cassius' plot, and that was Marcus Brutus. The name Brutus had a proud place in Roman history. A statue of Brutus the Liberator could be seen up on the Capitol, sword in hand, in memory of the great day nearly five hundred years earlier when the first Brutus aroused the Roman people to drive out their last king and found the republic. The Marcus Brutus of Caesar's day was, by contrast, a quiet, bookish man—and one whom Caesar loved as if he were his son. At Pharsalus, where Marcus fought in Pompey's camp, Caesar commanded his lieutenants to let no harm come to him. If they could take him without drawing blood, they were to bring him before Caesar—but they should sooner let him get away than so much as graze his skin. Brutus escaped, not knowing that his life was under Caesar's own protection. Soon after, they met fact to face, and from then on, Caesar showered him with favors, and entrusted to him the highest offices of state. But now, in March 44 B.C., Marcus Brutus was making plans with Cassius and more than sixty members of the Senate to take Caesar's life.

On the seventeenth day of March, Caesar would leave on the Parthian expedition, to be gone for years. Time was pressing. But Caesar's legionnaires were beginning to drift into the city from all over Italy, preparing for the great campaign. Daily, it grew harder to find their general unattended.

Then Caesar announced that he would meet with the assembled Senate two days before his leaving, on March 15—the day that the Romans called the Ides of March. This was the signal for his murderers. Caesar would come to the Senate unattended—and there they, Senators and officers of state, could gather and close in on him without suspicion.

The evening before the Ides of March, Caesar was dining with his friend Lepidus. Among the guests was another member of the Brutus family—Decimus, who had led Caesar's fleet to victory over the Bretons, and who had served his general well all through the civil war. The talk turned to the question of how a Roman would want to die. "Let death be quick," said Caesar, "and unexpected." Soon the guests retired for the night—Caesar without a thought for his own safety, Decimus pondering how he would kill him the next day. "Among the murderers of Caesar," Seneca dryly wrote after the deed was done, "there were more of his friends than of his enemies."

These friends of Caesar came together the next day under the colonnade of Pompey's theater, next to the chamber where the Senate was to meet. Cassius was there, and the two Cascas. Cimber had come, whom Caesar had made governor of the Black Sea province, and Trebonius, whom he had raised to consul not six months before. In the adjoining gallery of Pompey's theater Decimus Brutus was looking after a troop of fighting slaves whom he had brought to watch the games—and to protect him and his fellow plotters with their swords if things went wrong. Marcus Brutus was ready for the deed.

The Senators had gathered in the chamber.

The hour for Caesar's arrival came. It passed. Caesar had not come.

Cassius grew restless. Had Caesar found them out? Cassius looked about, then motioned to Decimus Brutus to go and learn what was delaying Caesar. The messenger was well chosen—Decimus was a man whom Caesar trusted blindly.

Decimus soon found him. Caesar had spent a troubled night, and was about to send a messenger to the Senators with his excuses and the request to postpone the meeting. But Decimus now gently took his old commander by the hand, and begged him not to disappoint the Senate and his friends who were all waiting for his coming. So Caesar was persuaded.

When the master of Rome, in his robe of state, entered the Senate chamber, the Senators rose in greeting and stood until he was seated on his chair of honor.

Now Cimber stepped up to him with a petition he had

carefully prepared for the occasion. The others quietly closed in on Caesar's chair from every side, daggers ready beneath their flowing robes. Cimber, as if in pleading, now laid his hand on Caesar's robe, tugged at it, drew it from Caesar's shoulder: the murderers' signal!

Casca, behind the chair, struck first. He missed his mark, only grazed Caesar's neck. Caesar shot to his feet and seized the dagger hand, and drove his writing stylus —his only weapon—through Casca's arm.

"How dare you, Casca!" he cried out in anger.

*They pressed in upon him, slashing each other in their haste to slay him.*

Then Cassius drove his dagger into Caesar's face.

Decimus' dagger cut into Caesar's groin, another into his side—another and another. Twenty armed men—or was it thirty?—they pressed in upon him, slashing each other in their haste to slay him.

Caesar fought—and though no longer young, he had his fighting strength: less than a year ago, at Munda, he himself had charged on foot into battle with his Tenth Legion.

And then, among his murderers, Caesar saw Marcus Brutus.

"You—too—Brutus?"

After that, Caesar spoke no more and fought no longer. He wrapped his robe about himself, covered his face, and through the crowd of his assailants he forced his way in silence toward the door. At the foot of Pompey's statue he fell, blood flowing from twenty-three deep wounds, and there he died.

So ended Julius Caesar, greatest of Romans.

His death threw Rome into a civil war more brutal and more bloody than any that had gone before, a war which laid waste the provinces and all but broke the empire in two. Most of his murderers died in the violence they had unleashed—their leader, Cassius, killed himself with the same dagger that he had stained with Caesar's blood. More than twelve years of carnage had to pass before Augustus, Caesar's grandnephew, gathered the reins of power that had dropped from Caesar's hand, and raised up the Roman Empire that Caesar's vision had foreseen.

Today his murderers are all but forgotten, or are remembered only for a deed that was brutal, cowardly, and useless. But Caesar's name lives on, for what he did and for what he was.

He was the unmatched master of the battlefield—and master of the pen. A single word from him swayed his rebellious legions. He knew no fear; he was forever ready to throw himself into the thick of battle, swim a roaring mountain river, or pick his way alone and in disguise through savage enemy lines. His mind was clear, and quick, and keen beyond the measure of most men. At every turning point in his life—in battle, in council, or in the seat of judgment and of power—we can see him making his decision, and taking action, with wonderful speed and still more wonderful justice. Better still, he staked his life on every one of his decisions, every one of his bold acts. He was aware, and he was unafraid—and so he was supremely free. Perhaps this fearless freedom of his mind and heart, even more than his great deeds in war and peace, is the reason why Julius Caesar has been called one of the few supremely great men in all history.

# BOOKS FOR
# FURTHER READING

Caesar, Gaius Julius, *The Conquest of Gaul,* translated
by S .A. Handford, Penguin Books.

Dodge, T. A., *Caesar,* 2 vols., Biblo and Tannen.

Duggan, Alfred, *Julius Caesar,* Knopf, 1955.

Ferrero, Guglielmo, *The Life of Caesar,* Norton, 1962.

Fuller, J. F. C., *Julius Caesar,* Rutgers, 1965.

Plutarch, *The Lives of the Noble Grecians and Romans,*
translated by John Dryden and revised by A. H.
Clough, Random House, 1932.

Shakespeare, William, *Julius Caesar.*

Suetonius (Gaius Suetonius Tranquillus), *The Twelve
Caesars,* translated by Robert Graves, Penguin Books.

Warner, Rex, *Young Caesar* and *Imperial Caesar,* Mentor
Books.

Wilder, Thornton, *The Ides of March,* Harper, 1948.

# INDEX